D1535355

Quilting and Braiding

*The Feminist Christologies of
Sallie McFague and Elizabeth A. Johnson
in Conversation*

Shannon Schrein, O.S.F.

A Michael Glazier Book
THE LITURGICAL PRESS
Collegeville, Minnesota

Cover design by Carol Weiler

A Michael Glazier Book published by The Liturgical Press

1   2   3   4   5   6   7   8   9

Library of Congress Cataloging-in-Publication Data

Schrein, Shannon, 1950–
    Quilting and braiding : the feminist christologies of Sallie
McFague and Elizabeth A. Johnson / Shannon Schrein.
       p. cm.
    "A Michael Glazier book."
    Includes bibliographical references.
    ISBN 0-8146-5876-8 (alk. paper)
    1. Jesus Christ—Person and offices. 2. McFague, Sallie-
-Contributions in Christology. 3. Johnson, Elizabeth A., 1941– -
-Contributions in Christology. 4. Feminist theology. I. Title.
BT205.S315   1998
232'.082—dc21   98–14894
                                                          CIP

For my parents
Clifford and Betty Schrein
who have always believed in me.

In a special way I dedicate this work to
Clara J. Barut.
You recognized the potential in me and
called it forth. You are a woman of
integrity, courage, and heart.

Contents

Acknowledgments

I am delighted to have the opportunity to formally thank the many people whose support has helped me to write this book. As the ideas for this work took shape I received valuable guidance and critique from my advisor and friend Bradford E. Hinze. He willingly read many versions of each chapter and offered helpful feedback.

My special appreciation goes to my colleagues at Alverno College for their academic and financial support, especially to those in the Religious Studies Department, and in particular to my friend and mentor Margaret Earley. Our conversations over coffee were just what I needed. Her confidence in my ability was a gift. Thanks also to my students whose probing questions have made me a better teacher, writer, and person.

I am thankful for the love and encouragement of my religious congregation, the Sisters of St. Francis of Sylvania, Ohio. Their wonderful influence on me, for more than thirty years, has imbued my life with rich Franciscan values.

Special thanks to my wonderful parents, my brothers Ron, Bob, and Dave, my sister Judy and their spouses and children. My family's support has meant a great deal.

Finally, I would like to thank my friends, Clara J. Barut who knew I was capable of writing this book, Michelle Kelsey who has always believed in me and whose honesty has kept me in touch with what is real, Bill and Sandie Roccia who are witnesses to me of the power of commitment and faith, and all those who have supported me by their friendship and love.

Introduction

At the heart of the Christian tradition stands christology, that theological discipline that deals with the person of Jesus Christ. Christology has been a contested issue within the short history of the feminist movement. Rosemary Radford Ruether in her work *Sexism and God-Talk: Toward a Feminist Theology* articulated the disputed question many women have asked: "Can a male savior save women?" In addition to soteriological concerns, feminists have challenged the ecclesiological ramifications of christology and its use as a warrant for the existing patriarchal structures within Christianity and within society at large.

It is possible to distinguish many strategies through which feminist theology has responded to this problem. These approaches have been broadly grouped into two identifiable categories. The first, revolutionary feminism, has abandoned the Christian tradition entirely in search of female religious expression (examples include Mary Daly and Daphne Hampson). These women have come to the conclusion that the patriarchal structures of Christianity and in particular the christological doctrines are irredeemable. The second strategy, reformist feminism, attempts to reinterpret and transform Christian tradition from within by searching the tradition for positive alternatives to the dominant patriarchal structures (examples include the subjects of this book, Elizabeth A. Johnson and Sallie McFague).

Though a variety of feminist theological methodologies can be delineated within the reformist category, I have selected two in particular, constructivist and revisionist, to examine in this work. I will explore the constructivist christology of Sallie McFague and the revisionist christology of Elizabeth A. Johnson as representative of the two positions.

Sallie McFague's work as a theologian is substantive. She has demonstrated her prowess as an academician and her commitment to contemporary liberal Protestant scholarship. It is clear that she has

1

come out of a particular movement in North American theology—constructivism—within which she is firmly situated.

Elizabeth A. Johnson has also produced substantive theological work. She has contributed a great deal of insight and solid scholarship to the academy while giving evidence of her commitment to Roman Catholic theology. Johnson's methodology is undeniably located within the revisionist movement in North America.

It seems appropriate to begin this dialogue and assessment by acknowledging the way in which each of these feminist theologians has adopted a metaphor to express her own position. Interestingly, both of these metaphors are drawn from practices that have been traditionally and typically a part of women's heritage: quilting and braiding.

McFague envisions her work as an important component of the whole enterprise, literally as one square of the quilt. The metaphor itself is one of construction. Johnson seeks to make a connection between what has been and what is now, enabling a new vision that provides the crossover in both directions in the form of a braided footbridge between the tradition and contemporary concerns, a metaphor of revisioning.

Constructivist Christian feminism understands the task of theology as that of a creative activity of the human imagination seeking to provide more adequate orientation for human life, essentially by way of the act of imaginative construction. Revisionist Christian feminism seeks to mutually and critically correlate the central and liberating themes of biblical and Christian tradition with the experience of women in the contemporary situation.

To bring these approaches into dialogue, this book will focus first on how Sallie McFague as a constructivist and Elizabeth A. Johnson as a revisionist address christological issues. Though both constructivist and revisionist feminists identify themselves with Christianity there is a fundamental difference in their interpretation and application of the christological tradition. It is this difference and its consequences that will be explored. Employing the metaphors of quilting and braiding, this book examines McFague's and Johnson's theological method and the particular way they understand the significance of religious language. Second, it carefully identifies their individual christologies; finally, it brings their christologies into conversation.

Chapter One, "'Quilting': Creating the Pattern," examines the evolution of McFague's theological understanding. Blending her study of language with her theology, McFague forges her early theology through the interpretation of parables within Scripture and tradition, making use of a hermeneutical method. In the second stage of her theological development McFague's focus on the use of metaphor results in the implementation of a heuristic method, the direct outcome of the creative moment of discovery experienced in every good metaphor. In her most recent theological work McFague identifies herself and her theology as constructivist. For her, the only appropriate way to respond to contemporary life is through the continuous construction of new metaphors that address, if only temporarily, the current theological needs. She images her contribution as the addition of one quilt square to the entire fabric of theology.

Chapter Two, "'Braiding': Formatting the Weave," explores Johnson's theological method and use of religious language. In an attempt to revision Christian tradition, Johnson "braids a footbridge" between classical and feminist theology. She returns to Scripture and tradition in order to discover the neglected or suppressed elements that appropriately respond to the theological concerns of contemporary women.

Chapters Three and Four, "'Quilting': Designing One Square" and "'Braiding': Weaving the Bridge," prepare the way for christological conversation by presenting McFague's and Johnson's christologies. McFague's theocentric christology views Jesus as the christic paradigm. The role of Christ is understood as giving shape and scope to the world as God's body, a metaphor McFague employs as a part of her ecological theology. Thus all creation is engaged in the process of salvation that takes place within the context of creation. Johnson's christology places Jesus Christ at the center of Christian theology. She focuses on the retrieval of wisdom, Sophia, as a means of responding to the christological concerns of contemporary women. Johnson seeks a liberating, inclusive christology that unlocks christology from the strictures of patriarchy and helps in the formation of a community of genuine mutuality.

Chapters Five and Six bring the christologies of McFague and Johnson into conversation. "'Quilting and Braiding' Christologies" probes the shared vision of these two important feminist theologians that includes their feminist perspective, their understanding of the significance of language for God, and their contemporary concern for ecological issues. In addition it assesses the implications of their theological methods and approaches to religious language in doing christology. Chapter Six, "Constructivist and Revisionist Feminist Christology," brings McFague and Johnson into conversation focused on the two central dimensions of christology, incarnation and salvation. Their individual approaches are assessed in relation to their impact on the whole of theology.

This book concludes with a brief epilogue, "Quilts and Braided Bridges," a reflection on feminist christology's contribution to christological study, and an assessment of the questions that remain.

Chapter One

"Quilting": Creating the Pattern— Sallie McFague

"Each of us is called upon to contribute one square to the quilt."[1]

Theological Method

Sallie McFague writes as a white, middle-class, American Protestant woman. She characterizes her position as "skeptical, relativistic, prophetic, and iconoclastic."[2] She understands her work to be *one* perspective among many and maintains that it is in conversation with other perspectives that limitations and inadequacies are recognized and consequently addressed. Each perspective offers a picture that, though it may be rich and full, remains a picture. Therefore McFague takes the position that "theology is *mostly* fiction: it is the elaboration of key metaphors and models."[3] McFague's methodological approach has evolved and changed over the years, so much so that there

1. "A Square in the Quilt: One Theologian's Contribution to the Planetary Agenda" in Steven C. Rockefeller and John C. Elder, eds., *An Interfaith Dialogue, Spirit and Nature: Why the Environment is a Religious Issue* (Boston: Beacon, 1992) 58.
2. *Metaphorical Theology: Models of God in Religious Language* (Philadelphia: Fortress, 1982) viii. For a critical review see David Bromell, "Sallie McFague's Metaphorical Theology," *JAAR* 61 (1993) 485–503; Ted Peters, "McFague's Metaphors," *Dialogue* 27 (1988) 131–140.
3. *Models of God: Theology for an Ecological, Nuclear Age* (Philadelphia: Fortress, 1987) xi–xii. For a critical review see B. Jill Carroll, "Models of God or Models of Us? On the Theology of Sallie McFague," *Encounter* 52 (1991) 183–196; Sheila Greeve Davaney and John B. Cobb, Jr., "Models of God: Theology for an Eco-

is only one identifiable link that consistently reappears. That link is metaphor.[4] Sallie McFague is clearly a constructivist in her methodological approach, though this was not always the case. An examination of the process by which her method has evolved will provide valuable insight into her theological position and ultimately will help to clarify her christology. Three distinct stages within her methodological development are apparent: hermeneutical, heuristic, and constructivist. Complementing the methodologies are three well-defined theologies: parabolic, metaphoric, and ecological.[5]

Parabolic Theology and Hermeneutical Method

McFague first elucidates her methodology in *Speaking in Parables: A Study in Metaphor and Theology* (1975). She focuses her theological reflections on the parable, which she recognizes as "a prime genre of Scripture and certainly the central form of Jesus' teaching."[6] McFague notes that the parable is an extended metaphor and therefore "metaphor is the heart of the parabolic tradition of religious reflection."[7] Metaphor is a part of ordinary language; it carries an emotional charge generated by the bringing together of the familiar and the unfamiliar. Not only is the metaphor emotional, but it is cognitive as well. It enables discovery, the learning of something new in the juxtaposition of what is similar with what is dissimilar. Thus, for example, in the parable of the prodigal son there is an unexpected turn of events when the father lavishes his wealth upon his wasteful son.

---

logical Age," *RStR* 16 (1990) 36–42; Elizabeth A. Johnson, a review of *Models of God: Theology for an Ecological, Nuclear Age*, by Sallie McFague, *Commonweal* 115 (1988) 151–152.

4. McFague notes the source of this consistent link: "[m]y interest in the relation between Christianity and literature arose in college when, as an English major, I began to investigate possible points of contact between these two most important facets of my life," *Literature and the Christian Life* (New Haven: Yale University Press, 1966) vii.

5. These three stages are reflected in the successive publications of *Speaking in Parables: A Study in Metaphor and Theology* (Philadelphia: Fortress, 1975); *Metaphorical Theology*, 1982; *Models of God*, 1987; *The Body of God: An Ecological Theology* (Minneapolis: Fortress, 1993).

6. *Speaking in Parables* 2.

7. *Speaking in Parables* 16.

Parables also bring together "the secular and the religious, our world and God's love."[8] These stories are about genuine people who live in the real world. There is a deep sense of realism within the narrative; however, McFague points out, "in the midst of the realism there is always an extraordinary and extravagant element, and it is this tension between the very ordinary and the very extraordinary that is the key."[9] It is the shock or surprise created by this tension that is the critical element of the parable and situates the metaphor at the center of the story. This unexpected turn of events or twist in the action is the revelatory aspect. McFague highlights this radical dimension of the parable as that which "provides the context which disrupts the ordinary dimension and allows us to see it anew as reformed by God's extraordinary love."[10]

This parabolic theology, which McFague at times refers to as story theology or narrative theology, is interpreted hermeneutically. McFague understands *hermeneutic* to mean "translating the word spoken in the Bible into the word for today."[11] The task is a "deformation, a recontextualization, of the tradition."[12] There is a clue to McFague's hermeneutical approach in the significance she attaches to the irreducibility of the metaphor. The form and content of metaphor are inextricably linked. In a religious metaphor, specifically the parable, the ordinary and the transcendent are so enmeshed that any hope of separation is futile. This fact underscores the need to return again and again to interpret the biblical symbols and thus necessitates a hermeneutical method. This carries a natural appeal for women who in revisiting and revisioning biblical symbols hope to unleash the power of female images that have been neglected or suppressed within the tradition.

McFague's emphasis on metaphor is an important element or "pointer" that directs attention to her eventual appropriation of a constructive methodology. She perceives this parabolic theology as intermediary, "a form of intelligence which is precise, discursive, and analytical, but also in touch with concrete experience and with the

---

8. Sallie McFague (TeSelle), "Parable, Metaphor, and Theology," *JAAR* 42 (1974) 632.
   9. "Conversion: Life on the Edge of the Raft," *Interpretation* 32 (1978) 257.
   10. *Speaking in Parables* 13.
   11. *Speaking in Parables* 30.
   12. *Speaking in Parables* 178.

imagination."[13] It is her openness to imagination and the recognition of its vital role in theological reflection that will ultimately lead McFague to move to a heuristic method, and beyond that to a constructivist approach.

Metaphorical Theology and Heuristic Method

The formulation of this heuristic method is laid out very carefully in *Models of God: Theology for an Ecological, Nuclear Age* (1987), but not before McFague shifts her emphasis from parabolic theology to metaphorical theology.[14] Metaphor is the thread that forms the warp of the theological fabric McFague weaves and will ultimately employ in the construction of her own quilt square. In *Metaphorical Theology* (1982) McFague continues with a hermeneutical methodology, but several factors shift the emphasis and propel her toward viewing the process heuristically. First, McFague delineates the meaning of several terms essential to a contemporary methodology. Second, her approach to Scripture and its authority is mitigated in that she no longer considers its authority to be absolute. Finally, she introduces feminism into the mix.

As she adds structure to her metaphorical theology McFague becomes more precise regarding the terminology she uses and the relationships between the terms. To her previous presentation of metaphor McFague adds an understanding of model. "The simplest way to define a model is as a dominant metaphor, a metaphor with staying power."[15] A model, though similar to a metaphor, reaches toward qualities of conceptual thought. A model is more comprehensive and provides an ordering structure while offering a wider range of inter-

13. *Speaking in Parables* 3, special note.
14. *Metaphorical Theology* 182. See also John C. Hoffman, "Metaphorical or Narrative Theology?" *SR* 16 (1987) 173–185; Egbert Schroten, "'Playing God.' Some Theological Comments on Metaphor" in John D. Woodbridge and Thomas Edward Cominskey, eds., *Christian Faith and Philosophical Theology: Essays in Honour of Vincent Brümmer* (Grand Rapids: Zondervan, 1991) 359–376; Frederick Sontag, "Metaphorical Non-Sequitur?" *SJTh* 44 (1991) 1–18; Janet Soskice, *Metaphor and Religious Language* (New York: Oxford University Press, 1985); David Tracy, "Metaphor and Religion: The Test Case of Christian Texts" in Sheldon Sacks, ed., *On Metaphor* (Chicago: The University of Chicago Press, 1979) 89–104.
15. *Metaphorical Theology* 23.

pretive potential.[16] From metaphors and models arise concepts and theories that are broadly understood as an "attempt to generalize at the level of abstraction concerning competing and, at times, contradictory metaphors and models."[17] McFague articulates the definitions of the terms and their relationship very succinctly in the following passage:

> By "concept" we mean an abstract notion; by "theory" we mean a speculative, systematic idea or thought; a theory organizes ideas into an explanatory structure. Concepts, unlike metaphors, do not create new meaning, but rely on conventional, accepted meanings. Theories, unlike models, do not systematize one area in terms of another, but organize concepts into a whole.[18]

Thus McFague identifies the continuum of religious language from primary and imagistic to secondary and conceptual.

Besides clarifying terminology, McFague takes great pains to communicate her position regarding Scripture. Scripture and its interpretation, though still undeniably significant, are no longer at center stage in McFague's theology. Metaphorical theology is open-ended and tensive. A metaphorical theology based on the parables of Jesus "will differ from traditional views of the authority of Scripture."[19] Metaphorical thinking views one thing in terms of another, refusing to allow those terms to collapse into identity. As a result the Bible, which is recognized as the premier metaphor of the word, "cannot be absolute, 'divinely inspired,' or final."[20]

The final piece that has a very direct effect on McFague's method and theology at this point is feminism. Her feminist critique alerts her to two potential dangers in the interpretation of dominant Christian metaphors and models: idolatry and irrelevance. One-sided patriarchal metaphors that have dictated the interpretation and expression of Christianity throughout the centuries are seen by McFague as idols. Becoming reified within the tradition, these metaphors are literalized and consequently are "dead metaphors." The tensive element of the metaphor has been lost along with the open-

16. Ibid.
17. *Metaphorical Theology* 26.
18. Ibid.
19. *Metaphorical Theology* 54.
20. Ibid.

endedness of the images. Along with this literalization of the models and metaphors comes the recognition that many of the images have become irrelevant, especially to persons who do not resemble middle-class males. Women, and all the poor and oppressed, are unable to find themselves within the Christian tradition.

In *Models of God* McFague refines her position regarding metaphorical theology. She sees it as a theology "at risk" because, in its use of the imagination, metaphor falls somewhere between non-sense and truth; consequently it always remains open to the possibility of being considered mere nonsense. It is because of the play of the imagination in metaphorical theology that McFague insists that it is necessarily heuristic. Since all language about God and God's relation to the world is inadequate, new models and new metaphors must be considered. Since new metaphors are not necessarily less proper than older, longstanding models and images for God this type of theology is destabilizing. This is critical to McFague's approach: she insists that "metaphorical theology encourages nontraditional, unconventional, novel ways of expressing the relationship between God and the world not because such ways are necessarily better than received ways but because they cannot be ruled out as better unless tried."[21] In light of all of this McFague defines a heuristic theology as one that "experiments and tests, that thinks in an as-if fashion, that imagines possibilities that are novel, that dares to think differently."[22] It is distinct from both hermeneutical and constructive theology and yet is similar. Hermeneutical theology is concerned with interpretation especially of the classic texts of the Jewish and Christian traditions as well as the theologies that have been derived from them. Heuristic theology is also interpretive and it is even concerned with the same subject matter, that is, the saving power of God. However, it is dissimilar in that it is not limited to interpreting classic texts or the texts of the tradition.

Heuristic theology shares some of the characteristics of constructive theology especially in its attempt to articulate God and God's relation to the world through a variety of sources including natural, physical, and social sciences as well as literature, the arts, and philosophy. According to McFague "it supports the assertion that

21. *Models of God* 35.
22. *Models of God* 36.

our concept of God is precisely that—*our concept* of God—and not God."[23] What makes the heuristic approach distinctive is that it will be more experimental, imagistic, and pluralistic. McFague goes so far as to call it "free theology," for it must play with the possibilities and consequently be willing to take itself less seriously. In an attempt to model this methodological approach McFague "plays" with the models of mother, lover, and friend in a remythologization of the traditional Trinitarian formula. Her effort, when judged by the criteria she establishes in her methodology, appears quite successful.

Ecological Theology and Constructivist Method

An equally critical dimension of McFague's theology is her attempt to do theology in an ecologically responsible manner. Hoping to achieve a holistic theology, McFague sets out four criteria for a contemporary theology of nature: such a theology must (1) be informed by and commensurate with contemporary science, (2) see all life as profoundly interrelated, (3) be creation-centered, and (4) acknowledge and press the interconnectedness of peace, justice, and ecological issues.[24] In a later essay McFague describes what she calls an "advocational theology," one that is not merely heuristic or merely utilitarian but is "rooted in the sense of reality current in our time."[25] It is a theology on the side of life and its fulfillment. This shift in focus away from the classics and the tradition to contemporary reality is the hallmark of her ecological, constructivist theology.

Throughout the course of her work McFague has placed more emphasis on construction as a way to do theology. In *The Body of God: An Ecological Theology* (1993) McFague shifts her focus to one image in particular, the universe as God's body. Embodiment appears as the most significant element of this model. Proceeding from the perspective of an ecological theology, McFague constructs this

23. *Models of God* 37.

24. "Imaging a Theology of Nature: The World as God's Body" in Charles Birch, William Eakin, and Jay B. McDaniel, eds., *Liberating Life: Contemporary Approaches to Ecological Theology* (Maryknoll, N.Y.: Orbis, 1990) 203. See also Clarke G. Chapman, "Speaking of God in a Nuclear Age," *AThR* 73 (1991) 250–266; Paul H. Santmire, "Toward a New Theology of Nature," *Dialog* 25 (1986) 43–50.

25. "Cosmology and Christianity: Implications of the Common Creation Story for Theology" in Sheila Greeve Davaney, ed., *Theology at the End of Modernity: Essays in Honor of Gordon D. Kaufman* (Philadelphia: Trinity Press International, 1991) 21.

metaphor in order to address what she perceives to be most critical in this postmodern age.

Religious Language

Metaphors, Models, and Concepts

There have already been several references to McFague's use of metaphor, model, and imagination, but for McFague the meaning and use of these elements are both critical, for she not only goes to great lengths to explain her understanding of these terms; she also uses them to accomplish her theological task.

In three major books and numerous essays McFague focuses her attention on the significance of metaphor for doing theology. She views metaphor as ordinary language, not the exclusive property of poets. Metaphor is so commonplace that ordinary language is replete with many "dead metaphors" such as "the arm of the chair" that have been used so much that they have lost their ability to shock or offer insight. Metaphor is used commonly to express things about which little is known or whose meaning is difficult to capture in language.

Metaphors and models arise from the imagination. In each new generation, believers attempt to express a portrait of God and to demonstrate by means of images the way God relates to the world. The primary task of metaphorical theology, according to McFague, "is the elucidation of an imaginative picture of the God-world relationship."[26] The kind of metaphorical theology she proposes "in focusing on the imaginative construal of the God-world relationship, attempts to remythologize Christian faith through metaphors and models."[27]

McFague defines a metaphor as "a word or phrase used *in*appropriately."[28] By this she means that it belongs properly in one context but is being used in another. To use her phrase, "metaphor is a strategy of desperation,"[29] for it is an attempt to say something about what is unfamiliar by means of something familiar. Metaphor has the character of "is and is not"; that is, there is a tension created by the

---

26. *Models of God* 92.
27. "Imaging a Theology of Nature," 206.
28. *Models of God* 33.
29. Ibid.

relation of similarity and dissimilarity. This tension is emotional: it is intended to shock, to capture the attention of the hearer, to lead to a new insight while at all times remaining open-ended. "Good metaphors shock, they bring unlikes together, they upset conventions, they involve tension, and they are implicitly revolutionary."[30]

Metaphor is particularly suited to religious language because of God's incomprehensibility and humanity's desire to know God. Metaphor provides a means for talking about God, for understanding God's relationship to the world, and for remaining open to new interpretations. All religious language is dependent on metaphor for its interpretation, for metaphors have the ability to create new meaning.

McFague is quick to point out the dangers inherent in the use of metaphor in religious language. Metaphors can be used so often that one gets used to them; when this happens they are no longer metaphors but traditional labels that swiftly become literalized. The metaphor is assimilated and the result is that "the shocking, powerful metaphor becomes trite and accepted."[31] McFague warns that "habit will always, it seems, triumph over novelty, no matter how shocking the novelty."[32] Similarity has become identity, "the metaphor becomes commonplace, either dead and/or literalized."[33] Such, she suggests, is what has happened with many of the traditional images associated with God. To call God father, for example, has become literalized through common usage, so much so that most people literally consider God a male. This concretization of an image leads quickly to a radical fundamentalism that refuses to consider that all language about God is metaphorical. Such refusal constitutes a form of idolatry.

The danger of irrelevance is also apparent in this example of God as father. In the experience of many women today this kind of image for God is no longer relevant, for it excludes half of the population and has been used to control and subordinate women for centuries. Its original tensive meaning, that God is as close to us as a loving parent, has been lost in the literalness of the patriarchal image. A fresh metaphor has the ability to spark imaginations. New possibilities for understanding God have the power to stretch the mind and heart.

30. *Metaphorical Theology* 17.
31. *Metaphorical Theology* 41.
32. Ibid.
33. Ibid.

McFague concludes that metaphorical theology, which is necessarily constructive, is the only appropriate task of theological reflection. She is convinced that in order to do theology "one must in each epoch do it differently."[34] This will involve risk, for each metaphor must be tested and its implications examined. Such a theology must be bold and constructive, for like a metaphor it must have the power to shock us out of our complacency and convert us to deeper meanings of who God is and the way that we relate to God.

McFague's metaphorical theology "attempts to consider the relationships among metaphor, model, and concept for the purpose of both justifying dominant, founding models as true but not literal, *and* of discovering other appropriate models that for cultural, political, and social reasons have been suppressed."[35] It is important here to clarify what is meant by a model.

A model, we recall, is "a metaphor with staying power."[36] It is more stable than a metaphor and has a broader scope that is capable of presenting a coherent explanation. Models are important because they are able to maintain the tensive function of metaphors.

McFague turns to models in science in order to illumine an understanding of models in theology. In doing so she recognizes four points regarding models that will help to clarify their use in theology. Briefly summarized, models: (1) provide intelligibility for the unintelligible, (2) are networks or structures of relationships, focused on behavior, (3) work in conjunction with theories to provide an ever-widening panorama of explanation, allowing for a connection between phenomena within a field and even at times across fields, creating networks, and (4) are paradigm dependent, created as well as discovered, and always partial.[37]

Despite these similarities there are several differences between models in science and models in theology. McFague identifies four:

> The function of theological models is comprehensive ordering rather than discovery; they are a necessity for meaning and explanation in theology in a more pronounced way than in science; models are ubiquitous in theology and related hierarchically as they are not in science;

34. *Models of God* 30.
35. *Metaphorical Theology* 103.
36. *Models of God* 34.
37. *Metaphorical Theology* 102.

theological models affect feelings and actions in ways scientific models do not.[38]

It is the role of the model, McFague claims, to be the unique union of primary metaphorical and conceptual language.[39] Concepts and theories arise from metaphors and models. A concept is defined as an abstract notion; a theory is a speculative, systematic statement of relationships. Concepts do not create new meaning as metaphors do; a concept is an idea or thought. Theories organize concepts into a whole.[40] In McFague's theological position "conceptual language tends toward univocity, toward clear and concise meanings for ambiguous, multileveled, imagistic language."[41] There is a symbiotic relationship between these terms, for concepts need metaphors and images to "feed" them while they provide "sight" for the metaphors.[42] The theological model is a unique combination of metaphorical and conceptual language. Many models are needed to constitute a Christian theology.

Returning to the metaphor McFague uses to describe her own work as a theologian, we can begin to see the construction of a unique quilt square that will be added to the cosmic quilt. The quilt, initially begun with a systematic pattern in mind, has evolved into what might be called an improvisational quilt. Each contribution to the construction of the whole is a reflection of the contemporary design that currently captures the imagination. One might say that it is spontaneous within an orderly system. The results are artistically dramatic.

38. *Metaphorical Theology* 107.
39. *Metaphorical Theology* 108.
40. *Metaphorical Theology* 26.
41. Ibid.
42. *Metaphorical Theology* 119.

Chapter Two

"Braiding": Formatting the Weave—Elizabeth A. Johnson

". . . this exploration attempts to braid a footbridge between the ledges of classical and feminist Christian wisdom."[1]

Theological Method

Johnson names her own position frankly: "I write in the context of white, academic, middle-class, American culture."[2] Born and raised in New York City, Johnson was educated through the doctoral level in the Roman Catholic tradition, which she acknowledges as personally and theologically formative. She names herself a second generation feminist who grapples with questions raised by feminist consciousness. As a reformist feminist she works within the tradition to bring about its transformation on behalf of women. She also wrestles with being a woman within Roman Catholicism, a tradition that dictates the limits of a woman's service.

Throughout her theological career Johnson has addressed the question: What is the right way to speak about God?[3] This question

---

1. Elizabeth A. Johnson, *She Who Is* 12.
2. "Redeeming the Name of Christ: Christology," in Catherine Mowry LaCugna, ed., *Freeing Theology: The Essentials of Theology in Feminist Perspective* (San Francisco: HarperCollins, 1993) 118.
3. The overarching question of Johnson's doctoral dissertation dealt with the nature of language and the right way to speak about God. "Analogy/Doxology and Their Connection with Christology in the Thought of Wolfhart Pannenberg." Ph.D. Diss., The Catholic University of America, 1981.

has naturally led Johnson to focus on christology, the heart of Christian tradition.

Critical Retrieval

The underlying presumption in all of Johnson's work is that there is wisdom within Scripture and Christian tradition that has been lost, neglected, or suppressed and that it is to our benefit as Christian people to retrieve these "pearls." Consequently Johnson begins from a historical and critical perspective in analyzing and assessing the truth contained within the story of Christianity. Johnson clarifies what she understands by the use of historical-critical methods especially as they apply to a retrieval of the historical Jesus, where "exegetes work methodically backwards from the written text, shaped according to the theology of the writer, through the mainly oral preaching tradition about Jesus which existed in the post-resurrection communities and on which the writers drew, to (with great caution) the death and characteristic teaching and behavior of the originator of that tradition."[4]

In her early work Johnson often dealt with questions and issues arising in relation to Mary, the mother of Jesus. She carefully differentiated between the nature of mariology and the nature of christology. Relying on the work of Wolfhart Pannenberg, Johnson points out that "Christology is the explication of the meaning of an historical event (the life, death, and resurrection of Jesus), while Mariology, possessing no such historical base, is the personification in symbolic fashion of the characteristics of the new humankind of faith."[5] Johnson's approach to mariology illumines her methodological technique. She neither dismisses the Marian tradition for its lack of historical foundation nor writes it off as simple piety. Rather, her stance is between these two extremes. Johnson carefully discerns the distinction between theological statements and historical statements when she interprets Scripture and the tradition. She is critical of any position that has not approached interpretation by means of critical methods of scriptural exegesis and the hermeneutics of dogmatic statements.

4. "The Theological Relevance of the Historical Jesus: A Debate and a Thesis," *Thom* 48 (1984) 5.

5. "The Symbolic Character of Theological Statements About Mary," *JES* 22 (1985) 313.

Johnson elaborates her methodological position by clarifying her notion of the "living tradition" and its significance for interpretation.[6] She suggests that there has been a false dilemma created through the juxtaposition of what is truly historical and the tradition or memory images that have been handed down in the Christian community. Instead she points to the significance of the position that respects and gives credibility to both elements.

Using the quest for the historical Jesus as the basis for her argument, Johnson first recognizes the fundamental importance of historical-critical exegesis of Scripture for delineating a correct interpretation of christology. She balances this position with a consideration of the memory of Jesus that gives shape to their understanding of him and as such has been preserved within the Christian community. The memory is a mediating symbol of the reality and mystery that is at the heart of Christian belief, namely, that God's goodness and graciousness are portrayed in the life, death, and resurrection of a member of our race in whom we have to do with the one God. This memory evolves and changes over the centuries, being shaped by the practice of the Church and the culture in which it exists. Thus the living tradition is composed of the historically retrievable facts and the memory of Jesus as it exists in the minds of believers and is handed down within the community. Johnson, in her own work, attempts to balance a critical historical retrieval with the faith confessions and faith images of the people of God.[7]

Waves of Renewal

Three waves of renewal in theology have washed over Johnson and profoundly affected her work: liberation theology, feminist theology, and ecological concerns.[8]

6. "The Theological Relevance of the Historical Jesus" 1–43.

7. See the following works by Elizabeth A. Johnson: "Mary and Contemporary Christology: Rahner and Schillebeeckx," *Eet(O)* 15 (1984) 155–182; "The Marian Tradition and the Reality of Women," *Horizons* 12 (1985) 116–135; "Marian Devotion in the Western Church," in Jill Raitt, ed., *Christian Spirituality: High Middle Ages and Reformation* (New York: Crossroad, 1987) 392–414; "May We Invoke the Saints?" *ThTo* 44 (1987) 32–52.

8. It is important to note that in addition to the contemporary movements cited here Johnson has also been profoundly influenced by numerous individual theologians, in particular Wolfhart Pannenberg, who was the focus of her dissertation, Karl Rahner, David Tracy, and Edward Schillebeeckx.

Liberation Theology

In the late 1970s and early 1980s liberation theology emerged as an expression of the voice of the poor and oppressed people of the world, beginning in Latin America.[9] Seen as a new way of doing theology, it drew on the experiences of suffering people who have been systematically oppressed. Naturally, the questions that emerged from this group of individuals gave rise to a unique methodology that has different characteristics than those of traditional theological reflection. Johnson highlights six characteristics of liberation theology.

First, "the context of liberation theology is the recognition of the suffering of a particular oppressed group."[10] There are a number of critical elements contained in this statement. The definition of a group as oppressed involves recognition of a number of possible reasons for the oppression ranging from race and gender to economics and ethnicity. In like manner the suffering will vary according to the nature of the oppression and the cultural and historical experience of the group. What is presumed in this statement is that the suffering of individuals under any form of oppression will give rise to a community in which the experience is shared. In the context of liberation theology this community has a shared religious experience as it becomes aware of its rage toward the oppressor and comes to terms with the belief that God does not intend the suffering but instead intends happiness for all people. As a result of this awareness the group is compelled to work and pray to change this unjust situation.

Second, "the reflection of liberation theology is intrinsically intertwined with what is called praxis, a critical action done reflectively."[11] Once one is aware of the injustice committed against those who are oppressed, the natural reaction is to take action on behalf of justice.

---

9. Johnson cites numerous Latin and North American commentators for her position on liberation theology. To name only a few: Victorio Araya, *God of the Poor: The Mystery of God in Latin America* (Maryknoll, N.Y.: Orbis, 1987); Jon Sobrino, "The Experience of God in the Church of the Poor," in *The True Church and the Poor*, trans. Matthew O'Connell (Maryknoll, N.Y.: Orbis, 1984); Roger Haight, *An Alternative Vision* (New York: Paulist, 1985); and Rebecca Chopp, *The Praxis of Suffering* (Maryknoll, N.Y.: Orbis, 1986).

10. *Consider Jesus* 84.

11. *Consider Jesus* 85.

Third, "liberation theology is highly conscious of the social nature of human existence."[12] This element of liberation theology recognizes that no one stands alone. In our goodness and in our sin we are relational beings. There is a sense in which sin, which affects the heart of the individual, is also social, affecting the community as a whole. To put it simply, when the rights of the minority are neglected, all people are ultimately affected. In contrast to the privatized view prevalent among the privileged, liberation theology highlights the sociality of human existence.

The fourth feature of liberation theology is that it "makes extensive use of social analysis."[13] Specifically, this approach uses social, economic, political, and anthropological studies in order to expose the cause of oppression and injustice. Its particular cast is taking the perspective of the victims and its aim is the restructuring of systems.

Flowing inherently from the preceding characteristics is the fifth, which names the goal of liberation theology as "changing the unjust situation."[14] Theology here intends more than the exposure of injustice. It seeks the liberty of all those oppressed.

Finally, liberation theology is impelled by the vision of "the reign of God, already arriving."[15] It is a form of realized eschatology, for the new heaven and the new earth are not only a distant hope but possible in this world, in this life. This vision has been initiated by the coming of Christ and will be carried out in the Christian community of faith.

What is the resulting methodology that issues forth from liberation theology? Johnson identifies three steps. First the oppressive situation is identified. This is a drastic change from a theology that accepts suffering as the will of God and looks longingly to a future release in death followed by entrance into heaven. It implies that complacency in the face of injustice is sin of its own kind. It calls for action and for embracing this life as gift from God to be cherished rather than spurned.

Second, Christianity is analyzed for what it may have contributed to the oppression. This is a soul-searching mode of operation

12. Ibid.
13. *Consider Jesus* 86.
14. Ibid.
15. *Consider Jesus* 87.

that demands a clear-eyed look at the root causes of injustice. This step involves asking sometimes uncomfortable questions and taking responsibility for the sin of the community. It means recognizing sin in all its communal forms, including sexism, racism, and classism.

The critical third step involves a look back into the Christian tradition through the eyes of the oppressed "for elements that would yield a new understanding and a new practice which would be liberating."[16] Liberating dimensions of the tradition are surfaced and reexamined. Very often there is a turn to the liberating actions of Jesus found in the gospels.

Johnson incorporates these elements into her retrieval of the neglected and forgotten dimensions of Scripture and tradition. Most profoundly, the view is from one particular group of suffering and oppressed people with whom she shares the injustice: women. One begins to see the intricate pattern of the braiding that will eventually provide the bridge linking classical and feminist theology.

Feminist Theology

One of the results of employing the methodology associated with liberation theology to interpret the texts and traditions of Christianity is the exposure of the patriarchal domination that has held sway within the tradition for generations. Whether prompted by the movements of liberation theology or simply as a result of personal experience as a woman of the Church, or by a combination of the two, Elizabeth Johnson has consciously taken up the cause of feminist theology and all of its ramifications. This conscious choice to align herself with the feminist agenda is apparent in a noticeable switch in language and emphasis.

In her early work on the question of God, Johnson refers to "the critique brought by women theologians against the exclusive centrality of the male image of God."[17] Two important issues are apparent in this statement. The first is Johnson's use of "women" instead of "feminist" as the adjective describing female theologians. The second is her distancing of herself from the project and questions of feminist theologians that are referred to in this context. In other

---

16. *Consider Jesus* 88.
17. "The Incomprehensibility of God and the Image of God Male and Female," *TS* 45 (1984) 443.

words, she does not include herself when she speaks of the questions and critiques raised by women theologians. The first clear reference Johnson makes to the feminist perspective is in an essay written in 1985,[18] yet in this essay Johnson continues to distance herself from the perspective of feminist theologians. While obviously well aware of the arguments and differing perspectives of feminist theologians, she still does not include herself in the position.

Johnson's ownership of the feminist theological perspective becomes evident in a short essay on feminist hermeneutics.[19] After identifying the alternative models, presuppositions, and strategies of feminist hermeneutics she concludes:

> As any number of feminist-minded scholars will admit, the effort to develop feminist hermeneutics is not just motivated by the desire to advance their scholarly discipline, although that in itself is legitimate. It is more an act of survival, motivated by the desire to believe in God in the midst of patriarchal society and Church.[20]

From this point there is a consistency of purpose in Johnson's work that is readily apparent. This aim is unmistakably articulated in her book, *She Who Is: The Mystery of God in Feminist Theological Discourse*. Her purpose in writing the book is stated unequivocally: "to speak a good word about the mystery of God recognizable within the contours of Christian faith that will serve the emancipatory praxis of women and men, to the benefit of all creation, both human beings and the earth."[21] In retrieving and ultimately revisioning the Christian tradition Johnson employs the strategies of feminist theology and liberation theology. Johnson applies the strategies of liberation theology to both Scripture and tradition in a search for ways to bring about an acknowledgment of the full humanity of women. For Johnson the

---

18. "The Marian Tradition and the Reality of Women," 118.
19. "Feminist Hermeneutics," *ChiSt* 27 (1988) 123–135.
20. "Feminist Hermeneutics," 135.
21. *She Who Is: The Mystery of God in Feminist Theological Discourse* (New York: Crossroad, 1992) 8. For critical reviews see Robin Darling Young, "She Who Is: Who Is She?" *Thom* 58 (1994) 323–333; Mary E. Hines, Mary Rose D'Angelo, and John Carmody, "Three Perspectives: *She Who Is: The Mystery of God in Feminist Theological Discourse*," *Horizons* 20 (1993) 339–344; Robert P. Imbelli, "She Who Is: A Review," *Church* 51 (1993) 51–56; Mary Aquin O'Neill and Mary McClintock Fulkerson, a review of *She Who Is: The Mystery of God in Feminist Theological Discourse*, by Elizabeth A. Johnson, *RStR* 21 (1995) 19–25.

measure of success in this endeavor "pivots in its fullness around the flourishing of poor women of color in violent situations."[22]

Seeking Alternative Wisdom

Johnson notes that when approaching the Scriptures liberationist feminist theology believes that "the core of the message of the Bible is one of God's saving liberation for all people."[23] It approaches the text with several basic assumptions clearly in mind. (1) For the most part the books of the Bible were written by men, for men, from a male perspective, in a socio-political culture dominated by men; (2) they pay little or no attention to women; (3) their later history continues in the hands of men within a patriarchal society and Church; (4) the word of God itself needs to be liberated from its overarching patriarchal bias.[24]

In the process of retrieving the value of Scripture for women the texts are examined for places where the story of women is present but has been neglected. Focus is upon the many passages in which women appear and their roles and functions as women of power can be discerned. The biblical message, focused primarily on men but read with the historical, socio-political and cultural experience in mind, can be universalized to include women. The Scripture is also searched for symbols and images that point to the significance and strength of women and for ways to liberate them from male domination. With the emphasis on women, the three-step method of liberation theology, "analyzing the situation, searching the tradition for what contributes to the oppression, and searching again for what liberates,"[25] is systematically used to reinterpret the scriptural tradition.

This critique also applies to classical theology, which Johnson defines as "the body of thought that arose in early Christian centuries in partnership with the Greek, philosophical tradition and continued through the medieval period, molding the discourse of the churches at the beginning of the modern era."[26] Once again the focus is on the full emancipation and flourishing of women. Johnson takes the total

---

22. *She Who Is* 11.
23. "Feminist Hermeneutics," 128.
24. "Feminist Hermeneutics," 130–131.
25. *Consider Jesus* 99.
26. *She Who Is* 9.

personhood of women with utmost seriousness and advocates women's well-being in all its dimensions.[27]

Following the pattern used to assess the scriptural tradition, Johnson applies the three-step process for accomplishing the goal of women's flourishing to classical theology. This critical analysis of classical theology is a deconstruction that "unmasks the hidden dynamic of domination in the Christian tradition's language, custom, memory, history, sacred texts, ethics, symbolism, theology, and ritual."[28] But deconstruction alone is not adequate to the task of raising up the full humanity of women. A second step involves searching the Christian tradition for alternative wisdom that will serve to accomplish the goal of transformation within the Christian community. The final step, then, is to reconstruct Christian theology, symbol, ritual, custom, and teachings in a way that will promote the genuine equality of women. This is the creative element of the process that renders new visions of the Christian community wherein all of humanity, as well as the earth and all that it contains, flourish in the wholeness and holiness of God's love.[29]

Ecological Concerns

The ecological crisis looms frighteningly before us. From a liberationist feminist theological point of view and methodology the exploitation of the earth and the reckless and sometimes cruel treatment of its inhabitants, not limited of course to human beings—in fact, all too often human beings are the perpetrators of these acts—is just one more example of oppression and injustice. To ignore this problem would be to contradict feminist and liberationist theology.

In the hope of ultimately creating an alternative vision Johnson parallels the injustice done to women "in the name of God" with the injustice perpetrated on the earth by human beings.[30] She argues that the "dominant form of western rationality called hierarchical dualism"[31] is a major contributor to the problem. This dualism divides re-

27. *She Who Is* 31.
28. *She Who Is* 29.
29. This constitutes a summary of Johnson's methodological process, outlined in *She Who Is* 28–30.
30. *Women, Earth, and Creator Spirit*, 1993 Madeleva Lecture in Spirituality (New York: Paulist, 1993).
31. *Woman, Earth, and Creator Spirit* 10.

ality into two separate and opposing spheres and assigns a higher value to one over the other. The result is a whole series of dualisms: spirit over world, human beings over animals, man over woman, rationality over emotions, the soul over the body, and so on.

Extending the method of the liberationist feminist model Johnson shows that it is possible once again to retrieve new wisdom from the Scriptures and classical theology regarding justice for the entire universe. In a revisioning of the role of the Spirit of God, Johnson moves theology toward mutuality within God, all species, and the Earth. The goal is a discipleship of equals with shared values of loving relationships and compassionate stewardship.

Religious Language

Symbol and Image

Johnson is keenly aware of the significance of religious language and its impact on the believing community. Her theological investigations often center on the appropriate way to speak about God and the difficulties encountered in attempting to name toward God.

The tension that exists is a result of attempting to use finite language as a means to name the incomprehensible God. She makes her position clear: "no human concept, word, or image, all of which originate in experience of created reality, can circumscribe the divine reality, nor can any human construct express with any measure of adequacy the mystery of God who is ineffable."[32] How then does one refer to God? Is it ever possible to express an understanding of the nature of God? Language for God relies on symbol, image, and analogy.

Given the broad interpretation symbol has had in the academy, Johnson focuses on one major position regarding symbol that is representative of the views of religious communities and academic circles, namely, symbolic realism. Drawing upon an essay by Lonnie Kliever, Johnson defines symbolic realism as the position "which understands religious symbols as non-literal representations of a transcendent reality, which so mediate reality that it is disclosed and communicated through the symbol and experienced in it."[33]

32. "The Incomprehensibility of God," 441.
33. "The Symbolic Character of Theological Statements About Mary," 320. Definition of "symbolic realism" taken from Lonnie Kliever, "Alternative Conceptions of Religion as a Symbol System," *USQR* 27 (1972) 91–102.

A critical element of this notion of symbolic realism is the stress on its nonliteral character. For Johnson, and most other feminist theologians, one of the major problems with interpretation of Scripture and classical theology is the literalism attached to male symbols and images that are used for God. Because, as Johnson frequently points out, "the symbol of God functions,"[34] it shapes the thought and language of the community of faith. When the symbol is God the Father, for example, and it is understood in a literal fashion, then quite literally God becomes a male in the minds and hearts of the people.

Johnson subscribes to the now classic description of symbol offered by Paul Tillich.[35] According to his analysis any true symbol has six characteristics. The following is a brief synopsis. A symbol: (1) points beyond itself to what cannot be grasped directly, (2) participates in the reality of what it represents, (3) opens up levels of reality that otherwise would be hidden, (4) arises from a dimension not under immediate rational control, (5) is dynamic, grows, and may die, and (6) points to what by its very nature transcends the world.[36]

In addition Johnson adopts the position of Paul Ricoeur in his discussion of symbolic language: "its structure is that of double intentionality by means of which the first or literal intent of a word carries a surplus of meaning which points through itself beyond itself to a second intent, analogous to the first but in a different dimension."[37] For example, the word "light" has a conventional meaning. When

---

34. *She Who Is* 4–6, 36–38. Johnson reiterates this phrase so frequently it serves as a mantra to remind the reader of the power, significance, and dramatic effect that the name of God has on humanity.

35. It should be noted that Johnson is influenced by numerous other theologians in her development of a theological understanding of symbol. To name only a few: Langdon Gilkey, *Naming the Whirlwind: The Renewal of God-Language* (Indianapolis and New York: Bobbs-Merrill, 1969); Karl Rahner, "The Theology of Symbol," *Theological Investigations* 4, trans. K. Smyth (New York: Seabury Press, 1974) 221–252; Avery Dulles, *Models of Revelation* (New York: Doubleday, 1983).

36. Taken from the work of Paul Tillich, *Systematic Theology* vols. 1–3 (Chicago: University of Chicago Press, 1951–1963); *Dynamics of Faith* (New York: Harper & Row, 1957); *Theology of Culture* (New York: Oxford University Press, 1959); "The Meaning and Justification of Religious Symbols," and "The Religious Symbol," in Sidney Hook, ed., *Religious Experience and Truth* (New York: New York University Press, 1961) 3–11 and 301–321 respectively, as quoted by Elizabeth A. Johnson, "The Symbolic Character of Theological Statements About Mary," 321.

37. "The Symbolic Character of Theological Statements About Mary," 322.

that meaning is associated by analogy to what is revealed in Christ the significance of light takes on a new meaning. It pushes the mind to a creative moment, one that offers insight. This symbol is then capable of giving rise to thought that interprets the meaning of the symbol. Characteristically, the symbol can never be dissociated from interpretation. According to Johnson "a symbol is a species of sign which carries a fullness of meaning going beyond what can be explicitly and exhaustively stated."[38]

Johnson interchanges the use of symbol and image in her theological language. She recognizes that images have the capacity to evoke the divine. Like symbol, an image points to a reality beyond itself. Image takes on particular significance when she deals with the notion of *imago Dei* and *imago Christi* in her theology of God and christology. Use of these terms is critical when applying the strategies of feminist hermeneutics to a retrieval of the Christian tradition.

Christian anthropology has traditionally maintained that humanity is created in the image of God and that we are transformed in the image of Christ. However, the Hellenistic dualism that was absorbed into early Christian tradition has caused a kind of ambiguity regarding the use of *imago Dei*. There was a gradual association of reason and rationality with men and thus with God, while bodiliness and passion came to be associated with women, relegating them to a lesser status. *Imago Dei* was interpreted in a variety of ways throughout history. Human beings imaged God in their stewardship, their soul, their will, their creativity, even in their righteousness. In each instance it was primarily the male who truly imaged God, women only secondarily through their association with men.

Johnson revisions the origin of this image in order to redeem it for women:

> Women are *imago Dei* in the exercise of stewardship over the earth and the capacity to rule as representatives of God, with ecological care; in their kinship by nature with holy mystery; in their rationality and intelligence and in their freedom capable of union with God; in their creativity, their sociality, their community with each other and with men, children, and the whole earth; in their bodiliness, their destiny. The wholeness of women's reality is affirmed as created by God and blessed with the identity of being in the divine image and likeness.[39]

38. Ibid.
39. *She Who Is* 71.

Regarding the use of *imago Christi*, Johnson observes that its association with men is based on a naive physicalism. Women by virtue of their bodiliness are seen to be different from Christ and therefore unable to be truly the image of Christ. Once again Johnson retrieves the understanding of this concept from the Scriptures with a return to its original meaning, that is, "that through the power of the Spirit the beloved community shares in this Christhood, participates in the living and dying and rising of Christ to such an extent that they can even be called the body of Christ."[40] Women as well as men through their baptism are *imago Christi*.

Analogy

While symbol and image are important in Johnson's theological work, analogy is of prime significance. It becomes a means for addressing critical questions about naming toward God. How does one dare to speak of God? Is it possible to deal with the limitations that are inherent in language? How is it possible "to prevent affirmations about God from being interpreted as direct transcripts of reality?"[41]

Johnson begins with the belief that religious language is analogical by nature. She draws this conclusion from a twentieth-century Catholic return to the historical sources, "accomplished in light of the exigencies of a contemporary mentality at once more skeptical and more searching."[42]

This Catholic return focuses on the work of Aquinas and his understanding of analogy. While we acknowledge that theologians continue to discuss and deliberate about Aquinas's use of analogy, it is possible to examine what he presents as the threefold movement of analogy and naming toward God.

Johnson presents this three-part movement of analogy very succinctly. "A word whose meaning is known and prized from human experience is first affirmed of God. The same word is then critically negated to remove any association with creaturely modes of being. Finally, the word is predicated of God in a supereminent way that transcends all cognitive capabilities."[43] The critical moment of this

40. *She Who Is* 72.
41. *She Who Is* 113.
42. *She Who Is* 116.
43. *She Who Is* 113.

action is the negation. This dimension of the analogical process keeps us from losing sight of the ultimate mystery of God. As Johnson applies it in her critical retrieval it serves as a critique of the literalization of any one image for God and as a reminder of what Aquinas so eloquently stated: "The names which import relation to creatures are applied to God temporally, and not from eternity."[44]

Johnson points out that for Aquinas "analogical predication rests on an interpretation of the doctrine of creation that sees all things brought into being and sustained by God who is cause of the world."[45] Using the analogy of fire burning wood, Johnson explains the relationship between the fire, here related to God or being itself, and the wood, representing every creature that exists. In much the same way as the wood shares in the being of the fire in its burning, so every creature shares in the mystery of divine being through participation in that divine fire. The result is a relationship of participation; "all creatures participate to some degree in 'being.'"[46] To the degree that creatures participate in "being" they can offer clues about the characteristics of God. Critical to this entire analogy is the realization that the fire is not the wood. By examining burning wood we are only given a glimpse into the nature of fire. In the same way creaturely qualities give us only a glimpse at God. Johnson concludes, "[t]hanks to the relationship of creation, words are but pointers to the origin and source of all."[47]

Johnson applauds the critical retrieval of this original sense of analogy that had been lost soon after the medieval synthesis was achieved. The Catholic return to historical sources has recovered the complexity of analogy, particularly the notion of negation.[48] The result is the fundamental recognition that the mystery of God will always remain beyond the grasp of our attempt to name it. In a sense

---

44. *ST* I, q. 13.
45. *She Who Is* 113–114.
46. *She Who Is* 114.
47. Ibid.
48. Here Johnson makes special reference to the works of Karl Rahner, *Foundations of Christian Faith*, trans. William Dych (New York: Seabury, 1978), and to David Tracy, *The Analogical Imagination* (New York: Crossroad, 1981). Tracy believes that analogical language is utilized by thinkers, religious and secular alike, and serves to enhance conversation. It is a recognition of similarity-in-difference that stimulates creative response.

there is a kinship, Johnson suggests, with the original reverential abstinence from the use of God's name by Judaism.[49]

Johnson maintains that "analogy shapes every category of words used to speak about God,"[50] metaphoric terms, relational terms, negative terms, substantive terms. In each case the same threefold movement must take place, affirmation, negation, and letting go in a transcending affirmation. There is always more meaning in the word or idea used than it can hold. Johnson claims that "analogy breaks this open in an affirming movement of the human spirit that passes from light into darkness and thence into brighter darkness."[51] Thus it becomes a critical dimension in any revisioning of Scripture or classic theology. In addition, it will profoundly affect today's naming toward God.

Johnson has braided together the intricate steps of liberation theology with the retrieval methods of feminist theology and the critical steps employed in the use of analogy. Together they form the braided and knotted strands that support the bridge of mutuality that enables the partners in this endeavor to critically examine each other's perspective in the visioning of their own.

49. *She Who Is* 115.
50. *She Who Is* 114.
51. *She Who Is* 115.

Chapter Three

"Quilting": Designing One Square—Sallie McFague

"The Christological question 'Who do you say that I am?'
receives a response with yet another dimension when
answered from the experience of believing women." [1]

For more than twenty years Sallie McFague has made significant contributions to theology. In that context her christology has evolved in tandem with her methodological approach. She has refined her constructivist method in light of an ecological theology and clarified her christological position in keeping with this perspective. McFague's christology—her understanding of the person, role, and function of Jesus of Nazareth—is discovered within the context of her overall theology. Unlike other systematic theologians such as Edward Schillebeeckx, Walter Kasper, and Jürgen Moltmann, McFague has not written a separate treatise on her christological view. Her position on the person, role, and function of Jesus of Nazareth must be drawn out of her theology. Her christology is paradigmatic and cosmic. It serves as a prism through which the Christian theological perspective can be understood. It is instrumental in determining a Christian morality and an overall understanding of the nature and experience of God.

Jesus as Parable

"The purpose of theology is to make it possible for the gospel to be heard in our time." These are the opening words of Sallie

---

1. Elizabeth A. Johnson, *Consider Jesus* 97.

McFague's book *Speaking in Parables* (1975). This statement establishes the context of her work and implies that her methodology is hermeneutical. She argues that theology would more appropriately fulfill its function if it were to focus on the parables of Jesus as models for theological reflection. The parables hold together language, belief, and life, thus avoiding the gap between thought and life, theology and personal experience. The parables also engage the imagination, a key dimension of McFague's understanding of theology. She states clearly, "One does not say 'Jesus is Lord' except through an act of the imagination."[2] It has been noted that "for McFague, theology is primarily a work of the theologian's creative imagination, a matter of constructing images and metaphors that are required by the demands of the present, as interpreted by the theologian."[3] McFague's exploration of parables will eventually lead to the development of the ultimate metaphor of the world as God's body. At this stage in her theological development, however, McFague acknowledges the parable as a "prime genre of Scripture and certainly the central form of Jesus' teaching."[4] What is unique about the genre of parable is that "the transcendent comes *to* ordinary reality and disrupts it."[5] Jesus is the ultimate expression of this experience: "to speak of Jesus as the parable of God: here we see the distinctive way the transcendent touches the worldly—only in and through and under ordinary life."[6] But what are the ramifications of this statement about Jesus? What is the christology that emerges from a parabolic theology interpreted hermeneutically?

The characteristics of the parable provide insight into this stage of McFague's christology. A parable is an extended metaphor. A metaphor is a common linguistic tool that is capable of conveying meanings that are difficult to grasp or put into words. The metaphor accomplishes this through bringing together the ordinary and the extraordinary, through the linkage of the similar and the dissimilar. The

---

2. McFague, "Imaginary Gardens with Real Toads: Realism in Fiction and Theology," *Semeia* 13 (1978) 241–261, at 251.

3. David A. Scott, "Creation as Christ: A Problematic Theme in Some Feminist Theology" in Alvin F. Kimel, Jr., ed., *Speaking the Christian God: The Holy Trinity and the Challenge of Feminism* (Grand Rapids: Eerdmans, 1992) 237–257, at 254.

4. *Speaking in Parables* 2.

5. *Speaking in Parables* 3.

6. Ibid.

tension that is created by this union has an element of shock. This shock is the springboard to a new insight; it is a revelatory moment. God is recognized in the ordinary events of life.

McFague finds that in the use of parable in the New Testament two new directions for religious language are suggested: indirection and extravagance. She sees them "epitomized in *the* parable of the New Testament, the story of Jesus."[7]

> Like a parable, the life and death of Jesus is a mundane, ordinary story raising in an indirect way through his work the question of his person. As with the parables, the focus of Jesus' life is on persons and the mode of their relations with one another and with God, epitomized by Jesus' relations with God as "father" and with others as brothers and sisters. Finally, the extravagance, unconventionality, and radicalism of the parables is reflected in Jesus' conflict with established mores and most acutely in his death on a cross which inverts expectations of the destiny of a "savior."[8]

The parable is also able to bring together the secular and religious dimensions of life. This is a special characteristic of parable, for as McFague notes, "there are no explicit statements about God: everything is refracted through the earthly metaphor or story."[9] So, for example, in the parable of the vineyard owner who chooses to be generous even to those hired at the last hour of the day the hearers are able to relate the generosity of the employer with the generous love of God toward even those who come to faith in the final hour. It is significant to be able to witness the power of God in the everyday. The question now becomes: what kind of christology is generated through this parabolic approach?

Jesus as the parable of God embodies the characteristics of an extended metaphor. In this way Jesus of Nazareth brings the extraordinary, that is, himself, into conjunction with the ordinary, the everyday life of humanity in this world. The result is a tensive shock or surprise, a revelation of God in the world. In Jesus the truth of God

---

7. *Metaphorical Theology* 44. McFague notes that there is widespread agreement (by C. H. Dodd, Norman Perrin, Amos Wilder, Robert Funk, John Dominic Crossan, and John Donahue, among others) that radicality, superabundance, or extravagance are the notes that set the parables off as different from poetic metaphors. Ibid, 204–205, special note.

8. *Metaphorical Theology* 53.

9. *Speaking in Parables* 16.

is embodied, expressing and communicating simultaneously. To know Jesus, to hear Jesus, is to know and hear God. This is God in human form; here is the surprise, the revelation, for God is enfleshed in humanity. The element of similarity and dissimilarity, which maintains the tension in the metaphor, is recognizable in the presence and hiddenness of God in Jesus. God is revealed and yet the fullness of God's reality is beyond the grasp of humanity. This is expressed exquisitely in the person of Jesus. McFague puts it this way:

> The belief that Jesus is the word of God—that God is manifest some-how in a human life—does not dissipate metaphor but in fact intensi-fies its centrality, for what is more indirect, "religious," than a human life as the abode of the divine? Jesus as the word is metaphor *par excellence*; he is the parable of God.[10]

The religious and the secular are brought together in the life of Jesus of Nazareth. McFague clearly states: "parabolic language does not take us out of everyday reality, but drives us more deeply into it, de-forming our usual apprehensions in such a way that we see real-ity in a new way."[11] Jesus did not call us from this world to another worldly existence. Rather, Jesus enables us to see the reality of life in a new way, with new eyes. The mundane world is transformed by the encounter with Jesus. God breaks into our everyday and that presence transforms lives.

Though one might draw the conclusion from what has been said that McFague's christology is very close to the orthodox understand-ing of Jesus as "fully human and fully divine," such a statement would be inaccurate. Her christology is "low" or from below, for the emphasis is clearly upon the person of Jesus of Nazareth as a vehi-cle for the divine. Perceiving Jesus as the parable of God necessitates flexibility and conceptual richness; even skepticism and uncertainty are appropriate, for a metaphorical statement is always a judgment of similarity and dissimilarity. McFague holds that "Jesus 'is and is not' God."[12] She is continuously aware that metaphorical statements are never identity statements. McFague is wary of idolatry and therefore will not make the move to identifying Jesus with God. This under-standing of Jesus and his role in salvation eventually comes to be ex-

---

10. "Parable, Metaphor, and Theology," 633.
11. *Speaking in Parables* 70.
12. *Metaphorical Theology* 51.

pressed in McFague's christology as the christic paradigm. If Jesus is understood to be a parable of God claimed by Christians to be true, then other religions can also claim to have metaphorical expression of the divine reality. To deny Jesus' identity with God is to send an invitation of participation to those who have been excluded by the particularity of Jesus: for example, to women who have felt excluded due to Jesus' maleness. A parabolic christology addresses the problem of Jesus' particularity while universalizing the God for whom Jesus is a metaphor. Jesus as the parable of God is McFague's christological starting point that leads her naturally to a metaphorical theology in which the event of Jesus' life becomes the paradigmatic event for Christian belief.

Jesus, Paradigm of God

A subtle but important shift begins to take place in McFague's theological reflection when she reckons with the knowledge that "theology is a constructive enterprise and . . . Christianity is but one religion among many."[13] First is the awareness of human construction in theology and its ultimate meaning for interpretation; second is the experience of religious pluralism that can no longer be denied on this shrinking planet. These two issues together propel McFague toward a metaphorical theology and a heuristic methodology for doing theological reflection. Rather than despairing over an attempt to identify the essential core of Christianity, she recognizes the advantages that result from this shifting perspective.

> The present situation, in which Christianity is not to be identified with an absolute deposit of sacred writings or with an infallible tradition of interpretation or with one particular set of models for divine-human relationship, is freeing the essential core of Christianity to live once again in people's lives. This essential core is not any book or doctrine or interpretation, but the transformative *event* of new life, a new way of being in the world that is grounded in the life and death of Jesus of Nazareth.[14]

13. "An Epilogue: The Christian Paradigm," in Peter C. Hodgson and Robert H. King, eds., *Christian Theology: An Introduction to its Traditions and Tasks* (Philadelphia: Fortress, 1982) 323–336, at 323.
14. "An Epilogue: The Christian Paradigm," 324.

This stance affirms the Christian way as a true way, but not the only way. McFague holds that Christianity at "its core does not dictate a set of beliefs but proclaims a saving event."[15] What is the impact of this position on her christology?

The concept of paradigm as exemplary formulation takes on significance in McFague's theology. She recognizes the appropriateness of its application to the theological formulations of individuals like Augustine and Aquinas, in the modern age to the work of Calvin or Schleiermacher, or even to broad movements like liberation theology. Ultimately all of these formulations make reference to *the* exemplar that is their foundation, the paradigmatic figure Jesus of Nazareth. McFague makes the claim that "what is paradigmatic in Christianity is the *event* of transformed existence associated with Jesus of Nazareth."[16] There is a clear emphasis here on event rather than on person. McFague suggests here that a broader definition of christology is needed, one that extends specifically to the events that were a part of the life and death of Jesus of Nazareth. Jesus, while remaining significant, is relativized in terms of Christianity. Here is the paradigm shift, as the events of Jesus' life are paradigmatic for Christianity but relativized in relation to other religious traditions.

McFague associates this theological perspective with four characteristic notes emerging in this contemporary situation:

> (1) the open relationship of Christianity to other religions; (2) the relative authority of scripture; (3) the oppressive nature of the hierarchical, imperialistic, patriarchal model for the divine-human relationship; (4) the emphasis on openness to the future rather than on the absolutism of the past.[17]

McFague's use of paradigm to interpret the story of Jesus of Nazareth is a response to these contemporary issues. It recognizes both the hermeneutical and the constructive dimensions of a heuristic methodology. The Scripture remains a resource, though definitely not the only source, for the story of Jesus of Nazareth. She also recognizes the partial and limited ability of humanity to interpret experience. She acknowledges the effect that culture, economics, and politics,

---

15. Ibid.
16. "An Epilogue: The Christian Paradigm," 326.
17. Ibid.

both historically and currently, have on interpretation. Instead of absolutizing what has come before, McFague uses the story of Jesus as a prism through which to view Christianity. She articulates her position succinctly: "To see the story of Jesus as paradigmatic means to see it as illuminative and illustrative of basic characteristics of the Christian understanding of the God-world relationship."[18]

Liberation theology has exercised profound influence on McFague's theology. She looks to the story of Jesus as destabilizing, inclusive, and nonhierarchical. In making a case for this position she considers Jesus' speaking in parables, his table-fellowship with outcasts, and his death on a cross.[19] From a liberation theologian's point of view "the parables illuminate the destabilizing aspect of the good news of Christianity; the table fellowship its inclusive character; and the death on the cross its nonhierarchical emphasis."[20]

It is not difficult to see the relationship between the parables and the aspect of destabilization. Recall that parables are extended metaphors and that metaphors are characterized by their shock value and their ability to hold the similar and the dissimilar in tension. Parables have a predictable pattern of orientation, disorientation, and reorientation.[21] The parable begins in the ordinary world with its common expectations. The story then introduces an unexpected turn or a radically different perspective than what might commonly have been expected. As a result, the listeners are challenged to reorient their thinking in order to accommodate the extravagance of the tension created by the parable. The parable has a destabilizing effect. It is intended to invert old ways of thinking. If this destabilizing aspect is extended to viewing all of life through the paradigmatic event of Jesus of Nazareth "it proclaims the end of the conventional, hierarchical, oppressive dualism of human/nonhuman."[22]

The destabilizing aspect of the parable is enacted in Jesus' table-fellowship practices. Jesus sat down at table with known sinners and outcasts of society. This surprising behavior was more than destabilizing to those who witnessed it; it was a challenge to be in-

18. *Models of God* 46.
19. *Models of God* 49.
20. Ibid.
21. McFague borrows this notion from Paul Ricoeur, "Biblical Hermeneutics," *Semeia* 4 (1975) 122–128.
22. *Models of God* 51.

clusive. Not only were the unexpected people invited to the table, but they were received as friends. The invitation is extended to all. The meal to be shared is one of joy and celebration. The model for the Christian community is one in which every person partakes in the table fellowship. The exclusive nature of past traditions and beliefs is shattered by this openness.

The experience of destabilization and inclusiveness is radicalized further in the cross. McFague notes, "the cross epitomizes the retribution that comes to those who give up controlling and triumphalist postures in order to relate to others in mutual love."[23] With this interpretation of the cross McFague makes a critical shift in her christology. From this assessment of Jesus as parable with the cross as a sign of the destruction of hierarchies she concludes that a triumphalist christology and a theology of atonement must be rejected. According to McFague the triumphalist christology of classic mythology with its theory of atonement is not appropriate in this ecological, nuclear age for three reasons. Briefly summarized, the classical mythology (1) insists that salvation rests with one individual and in one past act, (2) assumes that sin is against God, that it is rebellious behavior against the King, Lord, or Father, and (3) supports metaphors and models of God antithetical to those needed for imaging the God-world relationship in our time.[24]

McFague concludes from this interpretation that Jesus of Nazareth manifests God's love for the universe in his life and death. To understand Jesus as the parable of God opens the door to many rich metaphors for expressing how this love of God is to be imaged and therefore understood. McFague acknowledges that this constructive phase of her theology began after she read Gordon Kaufman's 1983 Presidential Address to the American Academy of Religion. "He called theologians to deconstruct and reconstruct the basic symbols of the Jewish and Christian traditions—God, Christ and Torah—so as to be on the side of life rather than against it, as was the central symbol of God with its traditional patriarchal, hierarchical, militaristic imagery. I answered this call, and my subsequent work has been concerned with contributing to the task."[25]

23. *Models of God* 53.
24. *Models of God* 54–55.
25. "An Earthly Theological Agenda," *The Christian Century* 108 (1991) 12–15, at 12. A student of Gordon Kaufman, McFague develops a theology of nature that at-

McFague puts her constructive, metaphorical theology into practice by conducting what she calls a "thought experiment" with new metaphors for God. To understand the expression of God's love through the paradigmatic figure of Jesus of Nazareth, she suggests the model of God as Lover.

God as Lover

God as lover is a part of a threefold model, God as mother, lover, and friend, that McFague suggests might appropriately serve as a "trinitarian" expression of "God's impartial, reuniting and reciprocal love to the world."[26] This thought experiment has been praised even by those who are critical of McFague's theology because of the bold nature of her constructive, heuristic thinking. Ted Peters notes that McFague's theology "is suggestive of new meaning or, even more boldly, in itself it is creative of new realities. Metaphors do not merely name things which already exist. They have the affective power to transform our consciousness and to evoke new visions which lead to new actions."[27] Within this model God as lover of the world "represents God as savior whose passion—both as desire for and suffering with the beloved—is oriented toward healing and reuniting all parts of the body."[28] This salvific love (*eros*) is the passionate manifestation, the incarnation of divine love. By this is meant that the beloved sacrifices all, goes to the limit for the sake of reuniting the world. This dimension of the model corresponds to the second person of the Trinity, Jesus.

Throughout her discussion of God as lover McFague is careful to keep in the forefront the nature of metaphorical theology, which is experimental. It does not produce dogmatic statements, but rather moves out of an imaginative boldness. The models that emerge do

---

tempts to reconceive belief in terms of contemporary views of the natural world (*Body of God* 65–66). There is a clear parallel to Kaufman's worldview that claims that any conception of the world must provide a background for and make sense of modern scientific knowledge concerning the developmental nature of the universe and the biohistorical nature of humanity. See his *In Face of Mystery: A Constructive Theology* (Cambridge, Mass.: Harvard University Press, 1993) 239.

26. *Models of God* 91.
27. "McFague's Metaphors," *Dialogue* 27 (1988) 131–140, at 134.
28. *Models of God* 91.

not claim to be true for all time but only for now. They are heuristic and limited.

The first question that must be addressed concerns McFague's understanding of the incarnation. This must be examined in light of her first model of God the creator as mother. "The model of God the creator as mother suggests an ontological (or cosmological) sacramentalism: the world is born from the being of God and hence will be like God."[29] The fact of being born of God, in God's image, is thus extended beyond the limitation of humanity to encompass all of life within the universe. God is incarnate in creation. McFague suggests that the world is God's body: that being the case, all creation is a sacrament or sign of God's presence. In this way McFague hopes to break down the ancient dualistic split of body and spirit and the hierarchical distinctions made between human and nonhuman life. But what about human beings? McFague sees the incarnation of God in creation as a whole and only secondarily in human beings, particularly those human beings especially open and responsive to God.

How, then, is one to understand the role of Jesus of Nazareth? McFague is very clear about her response to this question:

> Jesus' response as beloved to God as lover was so open and thorough that his life and death were revelatory of God's great love for the world. His illumination of that love as inclusive of the last and the least, as embracing and valuing the outcast, is paradigmatic of God the lover but is not unique. This means that Jesus is not ontologically different from other paradigmatic figures either in our tradition or in other religious traditions who manifest in word and deed the love of God for the world. He is special to us as our foundational figure: he is our historical choice as the premier paradigm of God's love. But all creation and all human beings have potential as the beloved of God to reflect or respond to their lover.[30]

McFague's christology is relativistic. It is reflective of a radical monotheism that influences her theology. Here the influence of Gordon Kaufman is apparent. McFague fears any form of idolatry, including what she calls "Jesusolatry." Kaufman fears reification: "taking the content of a symbol (or image or word) to be a proper description or exact representation of a particular reality or being; in

29. *Models of God* 135.
30. *Models of God* 136.

Kant's apt phrase, it is 'treating our thoughts as things.'"[31] There are many manifestations of God's revelatory love in the world, but no unique divine incarnation is needed, for God is incarnate as mother, lover, and friend in all of creation.

McFague identifies saving as the activity of God as Lover and healing as the ethical stance. The love that is witnessed in God as lover values the beloved. It is a love that is inspired by passion for the beloved and driven by a desire for union. What arises from this model is an understanding of salvation as union between the lover and the beloved. Separation and alienation are assumed; what is needed is reunification. In this model salvation is understood as "making whole or uniting with what is attractive and valuable, rather than the rescuing of what is sinful and worthless."[32]

It is impossible to consider the meaning and ramifications of salvation without considering the nature of sin and evil. McFague maintains that an ecological perspective affects the common understanding of sin. Sin must be understood in the context of the entire universe. Sin is the opposite of the hoped-for valuing of all life. It is understood as a turning away not only from God but from all of life. In the context of the model of God as lover "sin is the turning-away not from a transcendent power but from interdependence with all other beings, including the matrix of being from whom all life comes . . . it is the refusal of relationship—the refusal to be the beloved of our lover God and the refusal to be lover of all God loves."[33] In this sense it is a desire on the part of human beings to control, or to maintain hierarchies that lord it over creation. This position of dominance is a refusal of the balance of radical interdependence. When this takes place, "the vision of fulfillment for all is perverted beyond all recognition."[34]

From this perspective salvation is an extension of creation, a "second work" of God. All that has been created is valued. Each person has a responsibility to be a part of salvation. It can no longer be perceived as the work of a lone savior who brought about salvation once and for all, for salvation is an ongoing work of God as creator

31. *In Face of Mystery: A Constructive Theology* (Cambridge, Mass.: Harvard University Press, 1993) 330.

32. *Models of God* 130.

33. *Models of God* 139.

34. *Models of God* 140.

and of every creature within this universe. Salvation is understood as an action of making whole again; thus the ethic of salvation, in the words of McFague, is healing.

The characteristics associated with healing make it an appropriate image for the work of salvation. Most significantly, the model of healing undercuts the body/spirit split in traditional views of redemption. The emphasis is placed on the body as a condition of well-being and only secondarily on the spirit. This model has the tendency to highlight what we share in common with other forms of life rather than placing the emphasis on what distinguishes humanity. It is seen by McFague as congruent with the attitudes and actions of Jesus who in his healing ministry understood the natural relationship between healing the body and effecting a healing in the spirit. Healing is an appropriate image for salvation in an ecological context. If healing is bringing about a balanced integration in all the parts of an organism, then to work for healing on this planet, within this universe, is to attempt to bring a balance to life. This cannot be accomplished without a consideration of all creation. It makes us responsible for all life on this planet and for care of the earth itself.

Healing has a dual emphasis on resistance and identification. By this McFague means that God as lover of the world resists all disease, disorder, and chaos in attempting to bring about wholeness within the body. At the same time God as lover is able to identify with those who suffer as a result of our lack of integration and our sin.

The saving and healing dimensions of the model of God as lover are not dissociated from the classic notion of salvation, but there is a significant difference in McFague's approach when it comes to the role of Jesus of Nazareth. She claims that "as revelatory and powerful as that life was and continues to be, it cannot stand alone as accomplishing salvation if salvation is seen as the piecing together of the fragmented body of the world in one's own time and place."[35] In this view we are in need of many saviors. Many individuals over the course of time, both Christians and non-Christians, have been paradigmatic figures who revealed in their own lives, and often in their deaths, such radical and inclusive love as the world has seen in Jesus of Nazareth.

---

35. *Models of God* 150.

Christic Paradigm/Cosmic Christ

For McFague the key to understanding her current theological position is embodiment. Using the metaphor of the world as God's body as her starting point she presents an organic model as a major contribution to theology in this age, for it unites us to everything else on our planet in relationships of interdependence.[36]

McFague does not see Jesus of Nazareth as the definitive revelation of God. She is vocal in her objections to what she terms "the scandal of uniqueness" for she finds it incredible that "the power and goal of the universe is known only through a first-century Mediterranean carpenter."[37] She is adamantly opposed to the belief that the creator and redeemer is available only in the thirty-year lifespan of a single human being. In her own words, "the claim is not only offensive to the integrity and value of other religions, but incredible, indeed, absurd, in light of postmodern cosmology not remotely compatible with our current picture of the universe."[38] The emphasis is not to be placed on the "uniqueness" of the claim but on two beliefs that emerge from it: the physical availability of God's presence and the likeness to ourselves.

McFague proposes that the image of the world as God's body is given shape and scope by viewing it through the christic paradigm. In the use of this language McFague has removed herself a further step from traditional christology. No longer is Jesus of Nazareth referred to as the paradigm of God, but now the term used is an adjectival reference to the role of Jesus of Nazareth. Though it might be legitimately claimed that the center of Christianity is Jesus Christ, he has now been sidelined. What does McFague mean by the shape and

---

36. *Body of God* x. See also Barbara Darling-Smith, "A Feminist Christological Exploration" in Ruy O. Costa, ed., *One Faith in Many Cultures: Inculturation, Indigenization, and Contextualization,* The Boston Theological Institute Annual 2 (Maryknoll, N.Y.: Orbis, 1988); Geoffrey Lilburne, "Christology in Dialogue with Feminism," *Horizons* 11 (1984) 7–27; Nelly Ritchie, "Women and Christology" in D. Kirkpatrick, ed., *Faith Born in the Struggle for Life* (Grand Rapids: Eerdmans, 1988) 84–97; Megan Walker, "The Challenge of Feminism to the Christian Concept of God," *Journal of Theology for South Africa* 66 (1989) 4–20; Leslie Zeigler, "Christianity or Feminism?" in Alvin F. Kimel, Jr., ed., *Speaking the Christian God: The Holy Trinity and the Challenge of Feminism* (Grand Rapids: Eerdmans, 1992) 313–334.

37. *Body of God* 159.

38. Ibid.

the scope of the world as God's body, and how is it related to the reality of Jesus?

McFague states: "from the paradigmatic story of Jesus we will propose that the direction of creation is toward inclusive love for all, especially the oppressed, the outcast, the vulnerable."[39] Thus it is love, viewed through the lens of the christic paradigm, that gives shape to the body of God. In a Christian framework all of creation is encompassed in a particular salvific direction. Consequently "we can speak of the 'cosmic' Christ, as a metaphor for the scope of the body of God."[40]

McFague has two important moves in mind as she lays out her perception of the shape and scope of the body of God. The first is to relativize the incarnation and the second is to maximize the incarnation in relation to the cosmos. The first consequence of using the story of Jesus as a focal point for giving shape to the body of God is a new emphasis on the importance of embodiment. In his time Jesus addressed the needs of those whose bodies were in need of healing. He reached out to the poor whose bodily needs were not included in the hierarchy of values of the day. In this day McFague sees nature as the "new poor." This suggests that along with the human poor we must consider that nature is also poor as a result of sin that devalues life in any form. This is in keeping with an ecological sensibility. McFague goes so far as to suggest that "redemption should be enlarged to salvation: redemption means to 'buy back' or 'repay' through, for instance, a sacrifice, whereas salvation means healing or preserving from destruction."[41]

McFague presents an interesting threefold system of relations in outlining the shape of the body of God:

Christic Paradigm		
Action	Effect	Construction
parables	destabilizing	deconstructive phase
healing	inclusive	reconstructive phase
eating	nonhierarchical	prospective phase
(table fellowship)		

39. *Body of God* 160.
40. Ibid.
41. *Body of God* 168.

This christological position calls for two responses from Christians who take seriously their solidarity with the oppressed: liberation and suffering. The first, according to McFague, demands action. It becomes the responsibility of Christian believers to work for the liberation of all who experience oppression in any form. This is not limited to humanity but extends to the entire body of God, the universe. Suffering will be the natural consequence of solidarity with the poor. As full participants in salvation, Christians undergo the inescapable secondary experience of suffering with those who suffer. The inevitable result of siding with the oppressed is "death on a cross." In this image of the Christian in full solidarity with the oppressed the incarnation has been relativized, for each Christian is an active participant in the salvation, reunification, and liberation of all the oppressed.

McFague concludes that the scope of the body of God as seen through the christic paradigm is the cosmic Christ. She understands the cosmic Christ to be the resurrected Christ, the Christ who has been freed from the body of Jesus of Nazareth. She is careful to make clear that she is not attempting a description of the resurrection. Once again she is employing metaphorical language to deal with this mystery. One direct result of this notion of the cosmic Christ is the relationship between creation and salvation. McFague writes, "salvation is the *direction* of creation and creation is the *place* of salvation."[42] In other words, the entire cosmos is moving toward salvation that will take place within creation. The second dimension of this metaphor is that God's presence is available to us everywhere in the cosmic body of the Christ. This places the experience of resurrection on the bodily side of life. Death is not the separation of body and spirit but the fullness of the presence of the cosmic Christ experienced in the body beyond the limitations of space and time. The incarnation is, indeed, maximized by this understanding, for God is revealed in all life and death.

Sallie McFague presents us with a christology that has been profoundly affected by feminism and ecology. It is carefully constructed by means of metaphors and models that address the postmodern situation in which we live. It is intended to destabilize our thinking and move us toward more inclusive, nonhierarchical ways of doing theology. It challenges and critiques orthodox traditions that for too long have gone unchallenged.

42. *Body of God* 180.

Sallie McFague's Constructivist Feminist Christology

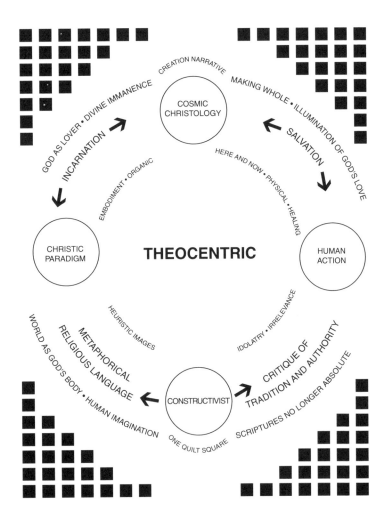

Chapter Four

"Braiding": Weaving the Bridge—
Elizabeth A. Johnson

*"This exploration attempts to braid a footbridge, between the
ledges of classical and feminist Christian wisdom. Throwing
a hermeneutical span from side to side may enable some to
cross over to the paradigm of women's coequal humanity
without leaving behind all the riches of the tradition that has
been their intellectual and spiritual home."*[1]

For Elizabeth A. Johnson christology is of central importance in
her theological investigations. It emerges in her work in three distinct
areas: within her mariology, as a part of her theology of God, and as
a study in itself including the closely related area of soteriology. Johnson's christology has been profoundly shaped by her liberationist
feminist theology. Currently it is being affected by her growing sense
of ecological concerns. Johnson's christology is most highly developed in the form of wisdom christology, in unison with the questions
raised by Christian women in today's church. Her christology pursues
a response to these issues that remains faithful to the heart and teaching of Christianity while opening the door to women's wisdom. To
use Johnson's own metaphor she "attempts to braid a footbridge between the ledges of classical and feminist Christian wisdom."[2] She expresses the hope that people may cross over to a new awareness of
women's wisdom and their coequal humanity without entirely aban-
doning the richness of classical Christian tradition.

1. Elizabeth A. Johnson, *She Who Is* 12.
2. Ibid.

The New Quest for the Historical Jesus

Early in her theological work Johnson lays the foundation for her christological position. Surveying the contemporary search for an accurate picture of the historical Jesus, Johnson examines its consequences for contemporary Christianity both within and outside of the academy. She understands "the historical Jesus" to refer to the image of Jesus of Nazareth reconstructed by inference from our present sources, using the tools of historical criticism.[3] Within the realm of Roman Catholic christology the historical Jesus has become an important factor recognized in the work of such theologians as Walter Kasper, Hans Küng, Jon Sobrino, and Edward Schillebeeckx. It might even be considered a primary catalyst for the interaction of systematic thought and biblical exegesis.

A caution has been raised by David Tracy about the theological importance assigned to this reconstruction of the historical Jesus. Tracy believes that "the historical Jesus is too fragile a base from which to make the Christian interpretation; rather, the personal faith response to the event of Jesus Christ along with and within the mediating realities of tradition and community alone provide the firm and constitutive foundation."[4] Tracy perceives the gospel tradition in Bultmannian style: it is primarily confessional and thus reflective of the experiences of the early Christian community. The predicament created by Tracy's question is how to deal with the historical Jesus and the memory of the tradition.

While recognizing the debate over the importance and consequent application of the reconstructed image of the historical Jesus within christological studies, Johnson proposes that this is a false dilemma. She advances a thesis that will ultimately serve as the foundation of her christological position.

> The reconstructed image of the historical Jesus not only functions today as the equivalent of the memory impression of Jesus in the early Church, but actually is the equivalent of it, i.e. is the means by which significant segments of the present generation of believers remember Jesus who is confessed as the Christ. As such, it is an element of the living tradition of the present Church.[5]

3. "The Theological Relevance of the Historical Jesus: A Debate and a Thesis," *Thom* 48 (1984) 5.

4. "The Theological Relevance of the Historical Jesus," 14.

5. "The Theological Relevance of the Historical Jesus," 25.

Johnson believes that the historical Jesus is not separate from the memory of Jesus held by the tradition. Rather, the historical Jesus is the foundation of the memory image, the referent for the confession that has evolved in the Christian community over the centuries since Jesus was on the earth in bodily form. The memory of Jesus has continually been transformed by the insights and life experiences of the believing community as it has been handed on to each generation. As such it has contributed to the content of the Church's belief, liturgical practice, ethics, preaching, and teaching. It has also been shaped by the culture in which the believing community exists. Thus it is passed on within the living tradition of the Church where the breath of new life through the power of the Spirit has been continually breathed into believing hearts. The exegetical search for the historical Jesus brings believers closer to the memory of the original witnesses. The image that results is not exhaustive of the actual Jesus, but approaches more closely the nature of his life and person.

Johnson notes the significant implication of this search for the historical Jesus. An examination of the life of Jesus profoundly affects the way one interprets discipleship. If Jesus is understood as someone whose relationship to God is as intimate as the use of *Abba* would indicate; if Jesus demonstrated a particular concern for the poor, oppressed, and marginalized people; if his ministry and life sketched a new vision of reality that challenged old classifications based on race, gender, or class; and if indeed Jesus died as a result of his fidelity to his mission, then living as one of his followers demands a response that may be quite different from the response called for in the past. From this Johnson concludes:

> [T]he Church's memory image of Jesus is theologically necessary for christology . . . the quest and its results have assumed theological pertinence not only for the correction of the distortions of the tradition (although certainly for that), but also for the constitution of the tradition insofar as it includes remembering.[6]

Johnson's concern is for the value of the "living tradition." Guided by the Spirit of God, the believing community expresses its faith. Two elements are of critical importance to that expression: all that has been historically given and its current form of reception.[7]

6. "The Theological Relevance of the Historical Jesus," 29.
7. *Consider Jesus* 2.

Faith is an expression of the individual and of the whole believing community. In this age we have inherited two thousand years of living tradition. The question of Jesus is posed to believers in every age: "Who do you say that I am?" (Mark 8:27b). Johnson fashions her christology out the insight that "debates over the interpretation of Jesus Christ are signs of a living tradition in the church which has moved with its faith out of a self-imposed ghetto into genuine dialogue with contemporary problems."[8]

Jesus, the Wisdom of God

Johnson initiated her retrieval of the significance of the gender of personified wisdom in the Scriptures as a response to the questions emerging from the growing awareness of the human dignity of women, an awareness that led to the critique of the androcentric nature of so much of classical theology.[9] Johnson recognizes that the initial response to the critique of patriarchal dominance in christology was a biblical and historical-critical search for the Jesus of history. She acknowledges that this process gave rise to an understanding of Jesus as liberator, one whose ministry was on behalf of the poor and oppressed, a ministry characterized by Jesus' conscious choice to liberate the captives and raise up the lowly.

Despite advances achieved through delving into the Scriptures and tradition in order to ferret out new insights into the humanity of Jesus, the gender of Jesus presents theology with the age-old problem of particularity regarding the one confessed to be God incarnate. In this contemporary age this particularity has been used in ways that are injurious to the dignity of women. Jesus' gender has been used to make God male by association. Even beyond a purely paradigmatic understanding God has been taken by some to be literally male. If Jesus, the incarnate word of God, is male, then the male human being

---

8. *Consider Jesus* 14.

9. Elizabeth A. Johnson, "Jesus, the Wisdom of God: A Biblical Basis for Non-Androcentric Christology," *EThL* 61 (1985) 261–294, at 262. See also Carole Fontaine, "The Personification of Wisdom," *Harper's Bible Commentary* (San Francisco: Harper & Row, 1988) 501–503; Amy Plantinga Pauw, "Braiding a New Footbridge: Christian Wisdom, Classic and Feminist," *Christian Century* 110 (1993) 1159–1162; Elizabeth Schüssler Fiorenza, *Jesus, Miriam's Child, Sophia's Prophet: Critical Issues in Feminist Christology* (New York: Continuum, 1994).

becomes normative and consequently alone capable of representing God. This line of argument has been used recently in official Roman Catholic teaching as a decisive reason for refusing to ordain women. Dissatisfied with the limitations that have resulted from christology that is based primarily on a retrieval of the historical Jesus, Johnson asks "whether it is possible with the help of imagery, concepts, and vocabulary of the wisdom tradition to think through a full christology which is faithful to the hard won insights of the tradition's faith proclamation at the same time that it breaks out of the usual androcentric pattern."[10] This question is indicative of Johnson's characteristic revisionist methodology. It is of critical importance to her that the insights of the tradition be maintained and re-visioned in light of the contemporary situation and explicitly in relation to women's issues. It is possible to image the footbridge as it is woven before our eyes. Her goal is a truly inclusive christology.

Scholars generally agree that there is a wealth of insight to be gleaned from the wisdom traditions found in the Hebrew Scriptures, the intertestamental literature, and the Christian Scriptures.[11] However, Johnson is of the strong opinion that the wisdom tradition has been relegated to a position of minor importance and that the figure of wisdom personified, *Sophia* in Greek, has been all but ignored. Johnson proposes that "both the insights and imagery of the wisdom tradition, when interpreted by means of a feminist hermeneutic, offer a way of speaking about Jesus the Christ that can correct the androcentric bias of traditional Christology and shape the community and

---

10. "Jesus, the Wisdom of God," 263.

11. See for example, James D. G. Dunn, *Christology in the Making: A New Testament Inquiry into the Origins of the Doctrine of the Incarnation* (Philadelphia: Westminster, 1990) 163–212; Raymond E. Brown, *The Gospel According to John, I–XII* (Garden City, N.Y.: Doubleday, 1966). Others have begun to demonstrate its relevance to feminist theology: Claudia V. Camp, "Woman Wisdom as Root Metaphor: A Theological Consideration," in Kenneth G. Hoglund, Elizabeth F. Huwiler, Jonathan T. Glass and Roger W. Lee, eds., *The Listening Heart: Essays in Wisdom and the Psalms in Honor of Roland E. Murphy, O. Carm.* JSOT. SS 58 (Sheffield: JSOT Press, 1987) 45–76; William Gary, "Wisdom Christology in the New Testament: Its Scope and Relevance," *Theology* 89 (1986) 448–459; Charles H. H. Scobie, "The Place of Wisdom in Biblical Theology," *BTB* 14 (1984) 43–47; Elizabeth Schüssler Fiorenza, *In Memory of Her: A Feminist Theological Reconstruction of Christian Origins*, (New York: Crossroad, 1983).

its engagement with the world in an inclusive, freeing, and relational manner."[12]

Johnson is careful to acknowledge that the wisdom tradition is not the cure-all for what ails classical theology. Much of the wisdom tradition came out of the same patriarchal mindset as the rest of the Scriptures. However, just as it is possible to discover insights for a more inclusive interpretation of other books of the Bible, so it is possible to critically retrieve images of wholeness from the wisdom literature that will benefit women and men alike.

Wisdom literature is distinctive from the historical and prophetic books of the Bible. It is more difficult to cast it into a specific, narrowly defined category. It appears in a number of texts that span a broad time line. It is not exclusive to Israel, but is also similar to writings emerging from Egypt and the Near East. Johnson points out that it focuses on "the continuing world of natural, everyday, mundane life, being interested in interpersonal and societal relationships, in nature and its workings, in the meaning of human life and the anguishing problem of suffering."[13] Wisdom is the necessary ingredient of daily life. There is a natural reliance on wisdom for the day-to-day decisions and choices that people face. "Since the whole world is God's creation," Johnson suggests, "life cannot be neatly divided into sacred and profane times or places but even in its dailiness mediates connections with the mystery of the Holy One, hidden and present."[14] Wisdom's connection with the everyday happenings in people's lives enables it to cut across cultures, ethnicity, race, and gender, thus making it accessible in the broadest sense to all of the created world.

Taking into account wisdom's breadth and depth in this world, it becomes profoundly significant that wisdom is characteristically personified as a female. Johnson emphasizes that "not only is the grammatical gender of the word for wisdom feminine (*hokmah* in Hebrew, *sophia* in Greek), but the biblical portrait of Wisdom is consistently female."[15]

---

12. "Wisdom Was Made Flesh and Pitched Her Tent Among Us," in Maryanne Stevens, ed., *Reconstructing the Christ Symbol: Essays in Feminist Christology* (New York: Paulist, 1993) 95–117, at 96.

13. "Wisdom Was Made Flesh," 97.

14. "Redeeming the Name of Christ: Christology," in Catherine Mowry LaCugna, ed., *Freeing Theology: The Essentials of Theology in Feminist Perspective* (San Francisco: Harper Collins, 1993) 115–137, at 122.

15. *Woman, Earth, and Creator Spirit* 52.

Sophia in the Scriptures of Israel

Johnson presents a detailed exegetical analysis of the appearance and roles of Sophia in the Hebrew scriptures.[16] In the book of Proverbs, Sophia first appears as a noisy street preacher who challenges the people to listen and respond with the promise that she will pour out her spirit upon them. Her words are those of a prophet and she speaks by her own authority (1:20-23).[17] In other places in the text, she plays an essential role in the act of creation, "the LORD by wisdom founded the earth" (3:19); she is "a tree of life" (3:18); she is the giver of life, "she is your life" (4:13).

Perhaps most significant of the passages on wisdom is Proverbs 8. In this second appearance as prophet she reveals much about herself. In 8:22-31 she outlines her direct participation in the act of creation. Sophia existed before the creation of the world and was active as God's major artisan in its design. Sophia describes her relationship to God as that of a darling child: "I was daily his delight, rejoicing before him always" (8:30). In her final appearance in Proverbs Sophia is the welcoming hostess who "has built her house . . . has hewn her seven pillars . . . has slaughtered her animals, she has mixed her wine, she has also set her table" (9:1-3). To all who eat at her table she gives length of days and "years will be added to your life" (9:11).

In the opening of the book of Sirach Wisdom is praised, for she is created above all and before all else; she is poured out upon creation (1:1-8). Later she is depicted singing her own praises and recalling that she alone has traveled throughout the cosmos seeking a resting place, eventually being told by the Creator to pitch her tent in Israel (24:1-21). She is even identified as Torah, the book of the Law that was given to Moses (24:23).

In the book of the Wisdom of Solomon, Johnson notes, the figure of personified Wisdom reached its peak of development.[18] Sophia is seen as having twenty-one attributes altogether, or three times the perfect number of seven (7:22-23). As an agent of God she has recre-

---

16. See in particular "Jesus, the Wisdom of God," 263–276.

17. It should be noted that Sirach and the Book of Wisdom are considered a part of the canon by the Roman Catholic, Anglican, and Orthodox traditions, but not by the Protestant and Jewish traditions.

18. "Jesus, The Wisdom of God," 266.

ative power and the power to save. To experience wisdom is to experience God, for she is "a breath of the power of God, and a pure emanation of the glory of the Almighty . . . a reflection of eternal light, a spotless mirror of the working of God, and an image of [God's] goodness" (7:25-26).

Johnson insists these texts be read within the context of monotheism. "*Sophia*'s functional equivalence with Yahweh requires that she be interpreted as a powerful female symbol of this one God."[19] To put it straightforwardly, the wisdom of God is simply God.

Though scholarly debate on the interpretation of personified wisdom remains unresolved[20] Johnson concludes that the most significant theological meaning that can be extracted from a close reading of these texts is that "wisdom is a personification of God's own self in creative and saving involvement with the world."[21] It is this understanding of wisdom that most clearly connects it with christological interpretation in the Christian scriptures. Johnson holds that "the tradition of personified Wisdom played a foundational role in the development of christology, and some of the most profound christological assertions in the New Testament are made in its categories."[22]

Sophia in the Christian Scriptures

Johnson concurs with James D. G. Dunn in his reading of the relationship between Sophia and Jesus Christ, "that Christ was (and is) the embodiment of divine Wisdom, that is, the climactic and definitive embodiment of God's own creative power and saving concern."[23] This conclusion is drawn from the direct relationship between Jesus Christ and Sophia that is demonstrated in the writings

---

19. "Wisdom Was Made Flesh," 99.

20. For surveys of the scholarly literature Johnson recommends, see Ulrich Wilckens, "Sophia," *TDNT* 7:465–528; R. B. Scott, "The Study of the Wisdom Literature," *Interpretation* 24 (1970) 20–45; Roland Murphy, *The Tree of Life: An Exploration of Biblical Wisdom Literature*, ABRL (New York: Doubleday, 1990); Carole Fontaine, "The Personification of Wisdom," 501–503.

21. "Jesus, the Wisdom of God," 273.

22. "Jesus, the Wisdom of God," 276.

23. *Christology in the Making* 212.

of Paul and the gospels. In fact Johnson feels certain that "early Christians tapped deeply into the tradition of personified Wisdom to articulate the saving goodness they experienced in Jesus the Christ."[24] In attempting to interpret their experience of Jesus and his saving actions Jewish Christians returned to the storehouse of images for God contained in Jewish religious tradition. It seems apparent that what Judaism said of Sophia, Christian writers now came to say of Jesus.

Paul is the first to directly relate Jesus with Sophia: "we proclaim Christ crucified, a stumbling block to Jews and foolishness to Gentiles, but to those who are the called, both Jews and Greeks, Christ the power of God and the wisdom of God" (1 Cor 1:23-24). Thus Christ crucified represents the wisdom of God and God's salvific action. In Johnson's retrieval of this wisdom tradition "the crucified Christ is the embodiment of God's wise intention to bring us to glory."[25] Once this explicit connection is made Paul seems to speak freely regarding the identification of Jesus with Sophia.

Paul is not alone in his assessment of the relationship between Jesus and Sophia. The Fourth Gospel and the Q document, a source for the gospels of Matthew and Luke, turned to the wisdom tradition to express the significance of Jesus, his life, death, and resurrection.

Q, no longer extant, is a postulated sayings source that presents Jesus as the sage whose words are wisdom. Jesus is understood to be the child of Sophia, the envoy who speaks prophetically but is rejected and murdered by the people (Luke 7:35). In Matthew's modification of Q the words of Sophia are placed in Jesus' mouth. In addition, Jesus' deeds are also presented as those of Sophia. Literally, Jesus is Sophia incarnate.[26]

In Johnson's view the fullest biblical flowering of wisdom christology occurs in the Fourth Gospel.[27] John appears to capitalize on the identification of Jesus with personified wisdom as it has already been portrayed in Christian tradition. Indeed, Johnson concludes that much of what distinguishes the Fourth Gospel from the synoptics can be attributed to its adaptation of the wisdom tradition.[28]

24. "Redeeming the Name of Christ," 121.
25. "Jesus, the Wisdom of God," 277.
26. In "Jesus, the Wisdom of God" Johnson presents a detailed analysis of the Q material and its relationship to Jesus.
27. "Wisdom Was Made Flesh," 104.
28. "Jesus, the Wisdom of God," 284.

The actions of Sophia are the actions of Jesus, seeking and finding, feeding and nourishing, revealing and giving life. Jesus, like Sophia, is identified with Torah, and he instructs his disciples in the truth. Jesus is once again portrayed as the embodiment of wisdom. Johnson gives assent to the conclusion of Raymond Brown's classic study, "in John, Jesus is personified Wisdom."[29]

The prologue of the Fourth Gospel presents a special case for developing the theme of wisdom and her relation to Jesus. Using the symbol of the *logos* (Greek "word") John "actually presents the prehistory of Jesus as the story of *Sophia*."[30] Johnson points out that the majority of biblical scholars agree that the figure of personified Wisdom has shaped the *logos*. The prologue is considered by some scholars to be a hymn coming from the genre of wisdom poems. It presents the figure of the *logos* in ways that strikingly parallel the presentation of *Sophia* in the wisdom tradition. Johnson maintains that

> The prologue to this gospel, which more than any other scriptural text influences subsequent development in Christology, actually presents the pre-history of Jesus as the story of *Sophia*: present "in the beginning," an active agent in creation, a radiant light that darkness cannot overcome, descending from heaven to pitch a tent among the people, rejected by some, but giving life to those who seek.[31]

From her study of the wisdom literature and its relationship to Jesus the Christ, Johnson draws four conclusions. First, the saving significance of Jesus can be understood in wisdom categories. The story of Jesus is the story of Sophia, the prophet and envoy of God who wills the wholeness of humanity. Second, the ultimate personal identity of Jesus can be understood in wisdom categories. Once the connection between Jesus and Sophia is made, the relationship of Father and Son that is most often associated with God and Jesus can be expanded to include the image of Sophia-God and her child. Third, the christological title of Wisdom can be given to Jesus, "Hagia Sophia, our Holy Wisdom, or Jesus, the Wisdom of God."[32] Jesus' life, death, and resurrection are associated with wisdom while

29. Brown, *John I–XII*, cxxii.
30. "Wisdom Was Made Flesh," 104.
31. "Wisdom Was Made Flesh," 104–105.
32. For these conclusions, here summarized, see "Jesus, the Wisdom of God," 291–293.

the significance of Jesus' life is expanded and deepened by its association with wisdom. Finally, *logos* texts in the Scriptures and in theology can be read through the hermeneutic of wisdom categories, so indispensably influential in their foundation. The result is that this type of hermeneutic highlights the inclusivity at the term's origin and creates the potential for a christology that is not intrinsically androcentric.

Jesus-Sophia

Johnson seeks a liberating and inclusive christology. Valuing women as full participants in the mystery of redemption remains the focus of her endeavors. In a move to achieve this new structuring of christology Johnson identifies several critical and interrelated steps: envisioning anew the foundational level, anthropology; respeaking christology by telling the story of Jesus as the story of Wisdom's child, Sophia incarnate; interpreting the symbol of Christ in a way that is faithful to its ancient inclusivity; explicating christological doctrine to release what is beneficial.[33] At the level of anthropology the problem is related to Jesus' maleness which has been interpreted as being essential to his redeeming christic function and identity.[34] As a result women are marginalized and their salvation is put in jeopardy.

Johnson locates the source of this problem within the ecclesial community. Males control the voice and the vote. To use Johnson's metaphor, "patriarchy is the bedrock for the androcentric construction."[35] Johnson envisions a different kind of community, one identified by relationships of mutuality. She seeks to be rid of the dualistic model that places women and men at opposite and vertical poles with the males commanding the top position and the women in subordination.

Choosing also to reject the limited position of a single-nature anthropology, Johnson suggests a way beyond both of these limited orientations: "one human nature celebrated in an interdependence of multiple differences."[36] Regarding humanity from a holistic vantage point, she views within men and women "a multipolar set of combi-

---

33. *She Who Is* 154.
34. Elizabeth A. Johnson, "The Maleness of Christ," in Anne Carr and Elizabeth Schüssler Fiorenza, eds., *The Special Nature of Women? Concilium* 6 (Philadelphia: Trinity Press International, 1991) 108.
35. "The Maleness of Christ," 110.
36. *She Who Is* 155.

nations of essential human elements, of which sexuality is but one."[37] This approach places sexuality into a more balanced position when examining the human person, rather than singling it out as dominant or more fundamental than any other human dimension. In this model diversity is celebrated as normal. Johnson presents a new anthropological vision. "Amid a multiplicity of differences Jesus' maleness is appreciated as intrinsically important for his own personal historical identity and the historical challenge of his ministry, but not theologically determinative of his identity as the Christ nor normative for the identity of the Christian community."[38]

In her rearticulation of the relationship between Jesus and Sophia, Johnson is dependent on the exegetical work of Elizabeth Schüssler Fiorenza who contends that "the Palestinian Jesus movement understands the ministry and mission of Jesus as that of the prophet and child of Sophia sent to announce that God is the God of the poor and heavy laden, of the outcasts and those who suffer injustice."[39] To use the symbol of Sophia to speak about the ministry and mission of Jesus is to shed light on Jesus' ontological relationship with God. Johnson makes clear that "none of the other biblical symbols used—Messiah, Son of Man, Son of God—connotes divinity in its original context."[40] To say that Jesus is the Wisdom of God is to say much more. The espousal of a wisdom christology is a declaration that Sophia in all her fullness resides in Jesus such that he is the manifestation of Divine mystery in creative and saving engagement with the world.[41]

The concrete life of Jesus-Sophia continues in the community of believers. The biblical metaphors of the body and the branches of the vine witness to the extension of the Christ event to the community. In the christological hymns the cosmic dimensions of the life and Spirit of Jesus the Christ are immense. Humanity is clearly *imago Christi*, but beyond that the entire universe itself is destined to be christomorphic.

---

37. Ibid.
38. *She Who Is* 156.
39. *In Memory of Her* 135.
40. "Redeeming the Name of Christ," 121.
41. "Wisdom Was Made Flesh," 107.

Not only does the biblical witness when reinterpreted shed light on the ancient inclusivity associated with the Christ figure, but the classical christological doctrines can be read in a similar way. In the debates of the first few centuries of Christian history the primary focus was on the humanity of Jesus. Scholars struggled to articulate Jesus' humanity and divinity. The controversy resulted in affirming that in Jesus Christ divine nature and human nature concur in one *hypostasis*. Johnson is quick to point out that "what was at issue was not his sex, race, class, nor any other concrete particularity but the completeness of his humanity precisely as human."[42] Ultimately Christian faith confirmed Jesus' genuine and complete humanity. It was not Jesus' maleness that was doctrinally important but his humanity in solidarity with all of humanity, making the focus of christological doctrine then and now inclusive. Gender is not constitutive of the Christian doctrine of the incarnation.[43]

The Saving Actions of Jesus-Sophia

In unlocking christology from the strictures of patriarchy, a wisdom christology paves the way for new interpretations of the death and resurrection of Jesus and the consequent saving effects of these actions. This interpretation challenges the way Christianity has traditionally understood Jesus' suffering, the role of God in Jesus' suffering, the purpose of the cross, and the expansion of the vision of who is saved.

As Johnson has clearly demonstrated, Jesus is the embodiment of wisdom. Sophia, the personification of God's wisdom, is the prophetic street preacher who comes to gather all God's people, especially the poor and marginalized. Jesus in his ministry and teaching is the street preacher who heals those who are in need of physical wholeness and offers loving compassion to those who are brokenhearted. Like Sophia, Jesus is rejected by those who are unable to hear God's call to an all-inclusive love relationship. In the end, Johnson notes, "the gentleness and inclusive care of Sophia are rejected as Jesus is executed, preeminent in the long line of Sophia's murdered prophets."[44] Jesus shares intimately in the suffering that is a

42. *She Who Is* 164.
43. *She Who Is* 165.
44. "Jesus, the Wisdom of God," 291.

part of this life. It is an identification with all who suffer, whether physically, mentally, spiritually, economically, or politically. All who experience the pain of injustice are one in the suffering of Jesus-Sophia.

In the Christian tradition the suffering and death of Jesus have been identified with the sovereign will of God. The classic tradition of the satisfaction theory of Anselm reasoned that God became a human being and died to take on what was due the honor of God offended by sin. Johnson calls attention to the fact that the satisfaction theory has come under severe criticism. She highlights four reasons. Briefly summarized they are: its focus on the death of Jesus to the virtual exclusion of the ministry and resurrection, its literalizing of what is meant to be a metaphor into an ontological transaction, its promotion of the value of suffering, exploited to maintain situations of injustice, and its effective history, which presents a picture of an angry God who needs to be recompensed by the bloody death of his son.[45]

Thus Johnson rejects Anselm's satisfaction theory. In a critical retrieval of the gospels she suggests that rather than a recompense for sin, the suffering and death of Jesus were a consequence of his faithful life. Specifically, she says, "feminist theology repudiates an interpretation of the death of Jesus as required by God in repayment for sin."[46] Jesus' death was brought about by an act of violence that went contrary to the will of God. In contrast to the satisfaction theory Johnson holds that Jesus' death "occurred historically in consequence of Jesus' fidelity to the deepest truth and love he knew, expressed in his message and behavior."[47] Jesus' actions often contradicted the Jewish law that existed at the time: forgiving adulterous women, eating with sinners and tax collectors, curing people on the Sabbath, proclaiming an intimate relationship with God. It was as a result of these deeds of Jesus that his life was required. The gracious God of Jesus enters into solidarity with all those who suffer and are lost. In Johnson's own words, "the cross in all its dimensions, violence, suffering, and love is the parable that enacts Sophia-God's participation in the suffering of the world."[48]

45. "Jesus and Salvation," in Paul Crowley, ed., CTSA *Proceedings* 49 (1994) 1–18, at 5.
46. "Redeeming the Name of Christ," 124.
47. Ibid.
48. "Redeeming the Name of Christ," 125.

Critical advances have been made in a postmodern interpretation of Jesus and salvation, and such work is raising new issues that are forming the frontier of soteriology today. Johnson recognizes that though much work has already been advanced, more is needed. She believes that the very framing of the subject at hand as simply Jesus and salvation is too narrow.[49] If the gift of salvation is the act of the Triune God, to concentrate on Jesus alone can lead to imperialistic action toward those who do not believe in Christ. In addition she thinks that the Spirit has received short shrift in today's understanding of salvation.

Finally, Johnson's revisioning of salvation expands the vision to encompass the whole world. Traditionally Christianity has held that Jesus came to save the whole world, but interpretation of that event has limited it to the salvation of human beings (and in most cases there is even a limit on which humans might be saved). Johnson recalls the words of Paul: "for the creation waits with eager longing for the revealing of the children of God; for the creation was subjected to futility, not of its own will but by the will of the one who subjected it, in hope that the creation itself will be set free from its bondage to decay and will obtain the freedom of the glory of the children of God" (Rom 8:19-21). It is not just human beings who are saved, but all creation. The ecological crisis that is occurring on our planet demands that our limited notion of who can be saved must be expanded. In Johnson's understanding of salvation, "we are of a piece with creation, sharing with all creatures a common destiny."[50] What is needed is a cosmic vision that promises salvation for the entire cosmos.

Johnson's revisioning of the wisdom tradition in response to christological questions has multiple ramifications. First of all, speaking of Jesus as Sophia, the wisdom of God, breaks through the gender barrier that has traditionally tended to associate the particularity of Jesus' maleness in an ontological manner with God.

In the second place, symbolism for God is expanded to include female images; thus the male Jesus is revelatory of the goodness of God symbolized as a female. Women are fully *imago Dei* and *imago Christi*. They share in the mission and ministry of Jesus.

---

49. "Jesus and Salvation," 10.
50. *Consider Jesus* 141.

Third, Jesus-Sophia became a human. In a retrieval of the spirit and intent of the classical doctrines it is absolutely essential that the full dignity of all human beings, women and men, become the focal point of the interpretation of the meaning of Christ's sojourn in this world. Jesus' embodiment in full humanity destroys the dichotomy between matter and spirit. Matter itself is connected to God.

Fourth, the use of wisdom categories is helpful in the ongoing struggle for the full emancipation of women and the formation of a community of genuine mutuality.

Finally, an expanded view of salvation, filtered through the wisdom tradition, refocuses the importance of Jesus' full ministry in an understanding of what brings about salvation. Jesus' actions are reflective of his fidelity to God and as a consequence bring about his death at the hands of those who were unable to accept the message. God is understood not as the vindictive, angry father who demands the bloody death of his son in payment of his honor but as one who stands in solidarity with all those who suffer as a result of injustice.

Salvation interpreted in light of the wisdom tradition gives rise to an expanded vision of who may be saved. A holistic picture of Jesus as savior of the world includes all of creation within the context of this saving grace of God. Johnson's revisionist wisdom christology critically retrieves an important truth of the tradition that has been ignored or suppressed and brings to light a model of Jesus that is at once liberating and inclusive.

Elizabeth A. Johnson's Revisionist Feminist Christology

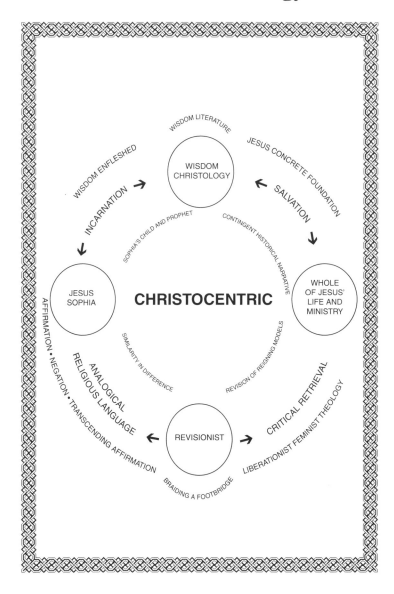

Chapter Five

"Quilting and Braiding" Christologies

"From the context of their diverse social locations, women call attention to aspects of Jesus' particularity often overlooked in previous Christologies."[1]

Shared Vision

Feminist Concerns

It is only acknowledging the obvious to say that both these theologians do theology from a feminist perspective. Each has made reference to the two groups, revolutionary and reformist, into which feminist theologians can be placed.[2] Both situate their own positions within the reformist group. Thus Christianity is perceived as a redeemable tradition that "contains untapped possibilities for revision of traditional theology."[3] The core principle of reformist feminist theologians is human liberation.

Johnson carefully articulates the meaning she associates with Christian feminist theology: it is "a reflection on God and all things in the light of God that stands consciously in the company of all the world's women, explicitly prizing their genuine humanity while un-

---

1. Mary Catherine Hilkert, o.p., "Feminist Theology: A Review of the Literature," *TS* 56 (1995) 327–552, at 343.
2. See McFague, *Metaphorical Theology* 152; Johnson, *Consider Jesus* 97–98. Both make reference to Carol Christ and Judith Plaskow, eds. *Womanspirit Rising: A Feminist Reader in Religion* (New York: Harper & Row, 1979) 10.
3. *Metaphorical Theology* 152.

covering and criticizing its persistent violation in sexism, itself an omnipresent paradigm of unjust relationships."[4] It presumes that women are equal sharers in the religious heritage of Christianity precisely as full and independent human beings and not as persons who are dependent on males for their identity. Feminism recognizes that the sin of sexism exists, and it calls for a full conversion to the recognition that all humankind is *imago Dei*. Finally, feminist theology "advocates the reform of patriarchal civil and ecclesial structures and the intellectual systems that support them in order to release all human beings for more just designs of living with each other and the earth."[5]

According to Sallie McFague reformist feminist theologians[6] believe that the root metaphor of Christianity is human liberation and that it is possible for the liberation of women to occur within the Christian paradigm.[7] Especially in her early work McFague places a great deal of emphasis on the feminist critique of Christian tradition as a means of moving toward the full liberation of women and ultimately of all humanity.

This feminist vision has established the direction that both McFague and Johnson take in beginning their work with a critique of the patriarchal dominance found in the Christian tradition. Each recognizes that the critique must be initiated with an examination of Christianity's doctrine of God. Their underlying assumption is that patriarchy has had a profoundly negative effect on the way theology is done. The result is the neglect and overt oppression of women.

Speaking About God

For Elizabeth Johnson the overriding question that directs all of her study is "what is the right way to speak about God?"[8] The key to understanding her approach is a phrase she repeats frequently: "the

---

4. *She Who Is: The Mystery of God in Feminist Theological Discourse* (New York: Crossroad, 1992) 8.
5. *She Who Is* 9.
6. McFague specifically calls herself a reformist in *Metaphorical Theology* 153.
7. *Metaphorical Theology* 164.
8. See in particular Johnson's dissertation, *Analogy/Doxology and Their Connection with Christology*, and *She Who Is* 3–16.

symbol of God functions . . . ."[9] There are obvious implications of this approach. God is the primary symbol of the entire religious system and as such is the ultimate reference point for understanding life and the world. Language is of utmost importance because the way in which a faith community shapes language about God implicitly represents what it takes to be the highest good, the profoundest truth. Speech about God shapes the life orientation of the Christian community and specifically of each individual Christian and directs its praxis. Johnson points out that speaking about God "sums up, unifies, and expresses a faith community's sense of ultimate mystery, the world view and expectation of order devolving from this, and the concomitant orientation of human life and devotion."[10]

Christian "feminist liberation theology," the position that Johnson takes in her critique, finds Christian tradition to be at once oppressive and idolatrous. It is oppressive because it draws its images and language for God almost exclusively from the "world of ruling men."[11] Human equality is undermined. Classical theism is idolatrous in the way it has absolutized a single set of metaphors, making male-dominated language the "supremely fitting way of speaking about God."[12]

In her critique of Christian tradition McFague's charges sound a similar note. She finds religious language in danger of becoming both irrelevant and idolatrous. Without consciousness of the interpretive context that recognizes that persons speaking about God are social, cultural, and historical beings with particular perspectives, and without a concern for this plurality of perspectives, language about God too easily becomes corrupt or useless. McFague suggests that "it will become idolatrous, for we will absolutize one tradition of images for God; it will become irrelevant, for the experiences of many people will not be included within the canonized tradition."[13]

Traditional theology, in particular language about God, has fallen into these traps in its use of male imagery. Its singular focus and narrow literalization of exclusive images for God has indeed

9. *She Who Is* 3–16.
10. *She Who Is* 4.
11. *She Who Is* 18.
12. Ibid.
13. *Metaphorical Theology* 3.

absolutized God as male and excluded half the world's population in its likening of God to humanity.

Ecological Concerns

Christian liberation feminism does not limit its critique to language. A critical dimension of this perspective is the position of the reflecting person, the theologian or thinker, as one of the oppressed. For McFague and Johnson the experience of oppression has developed a sensitivity to and for all who have been affected by the dominance of one group over another. One obvious consequence is an ecological concern.

Ecological issues arise from concern over humanity's careless regard for the earth and all the life it supports. McFague has made some bold new moves in addressing this concern. She considers Christian theology from the perspective of an organic model of embodiment, specifically of the universe as God's body. Johnson addresses these questions also. She offers a creative look at the relationship between the way women have been traditionally treated within Christianity, the way that humanity has treated the earth, and the way that Christian theology has all but neglected the role and function of the Holy Spirit. In her presidential address to the Catholic Theological Society of America Johnson pointed out that ". . . as theologians of the twenty-first century, we need to complete our recent anthropological turns by turning to the entire interconnected community of life and the network of life-systems in which the human race is embedded, all of which has its own intrinsic value before God."[14]

Beginning the Conversation

Methodology

Operating within the methodological framework that believes that all of theology is constructive, Sallie McFague first of all maintains that "different imagery is needed in order to express Christian

---

14. "Turn to the Heavens and the Earth: Retrieval of the Cosmos in Theology," CTSA *Proceedings* 51 (1996) 1–14, at 1.

transformation in different times."[15] The presumption here is that in each new age the task of theology is to construct images that are capable of expressing God's relationship to the world. Secondary to this assumption is the proposition that images and metaphors, which were at one time helpful in expressing the nature of God's relationship to the world, are not necessarily still adequate or even correct when used today.

This leads to a second assumption: all images and metaphors for God must be critically analyzed from a contemporary perspective and those found to be no longer relevant and useful for addressing today's concerns and expressing an appropriate understanding of who God is should be discarded.

A third assumption involves the critical role of theologians. Within this framework the theologian is responsible for good critical analysis of theological constructions past and present. The theologian is also responsible for the construction of new models that respond to current needs.

Johnson's methodological framework is undergirded by a different set of assumptions. The most obvious is that the Christian tradition is in need of revision. Specifically, the question Johnson asks is "whether, when read with a feminist hermeneutic, there is anything in the classical tradition in all of its vastness that could serve a discourse about divine mystery that would further the emancipation of women."[16] Implied within this question is a second assumption, that the tradition is redeemable. The specific task of the theologian is thus defined: to examine the tradition through the lens of liberation feminism, looking for the "hidden" or neglected wisdom concerning women. Johnson hopes to accomplish a critical retrieval in the light of women's coequal humanity.

Assessment

A subtle difference in approach emerges from this probe of McFague's and Johnson's methodological assumptions. The difference is in their expectations. McFague approaches critical analysis of traditional Christian formulations with the expectation that they will

---

15. "The World as God's Body," *The Christian Century* 105 (1988) 671.
16. *She Who Is* 9.

no longer be relevant to contemporary matters. She is willing to discard them; in fact she insists that they be discarded in favor of new constructions that do address the needs of today. Johnson's expectation is that what is needed to bring about women and men's coequal humanity lies hidden or suppressed within the tradition.

The role or task of the theologian is also perceived differently. Within the constructivist framework the theologian goes about the task of critical analysis with an eye to removing or discarding formulations that are perceived to be irrelevant. In addition theologians are required to make use of all their creative and imagistic energies for the creation of new metaphors and models that will meet the needs of the contemporary world. In this way the theologian is both poet and philosopher. As poet the theologian is sensitive to the metaphors and images that express Christian faith for our day; as philosopher the theologian articulates in a coherent and systematic fashion the interpretation and implication of these metaphors and images. McFague resolutely states, "I believe our time is sufficiently different and sufficiently dire that theologians must not shrink from the task of thinking boldly and imaginatively."[17]

On the other hand the revisionist theologian will bring her or his creative energies to bear on re-creating and re-visioning the Christian tradition in an act of retrieval. To return to Johnson's metaphor of braiding a footbridge, the theologian is engaged in making connections between past and present Christian issues for the sake of a secure future. This is not meant to suggest that constructive theologians use their creative imaginations and revisionist theologians do not. Rather it is the perspective and stance from which the theologizing takes place that differentiates the methodologies. Constructivists are focused on the present and the future. The past traditions serve a purpose only in the sense that they can be used to serve the contemporary moment. Theologians employ their creativity in order to create new images and understandings for God.

In contrast, revisionists not only make use of creative imagination to create new images for speaking about God. They also use that same creative energy to retrieve images from the past tradition that have been neglected, suppressed, or interpreted differently. The focus

17. *Models of God* 29.

is on bridging the gap between the past and the future while addressing the concerns of the present moment.

This image of braiding the footbridge suggests what some might judge to be a weakness within the revisionist methodology, namely the establishing of an external boundary that confines the conversation to the realm of Christianity, creating a kind of "closed loop" system of evaluation. However, allowing the questions of feminist Christian wisdom to engage classical theism and vice versa provides a model of mutuality that enhances the view from both sides of the bridge. The contemporary concerns of the culture, in particular of feminism, seek their place within the Christian tradition and classical theism is internally renewed in its response. To put it in Johnson's own words, "throwing a hermeneutical span from side to side may enable some to cross over to the paradigm of women's coequal humanity without leaving behind all the riches of the tradition that has been their intellectual and spiritual home."[18]

Constructivism, in contrast, has an open-ended, evolutionary trajectory. Its concern is to address the issues of each new age; it is not confined by the limitations of the past. To use McFague's metaphor, new squares can be added to the whole quilt at any time. In fact, new creative images are required as the needs within this age expand, change, and call for new directions. The problem, however, has to do with direction. All of classical theism, including the biblical witness, is critiqued and analyzed from the position of our day. Contemporary concerns and needs are the measure for holding on to or discarding biblical and traditional Christian symbols, and images. The reverse is not true. Contemporary concerns are not examined in light of the teaching and wisdom of Christian truths. The model is not balanced. The danger is the loss of traditional wisdom.

Religious Language

McFague suggests that all language about God lies somewhere between truth and fiction. Since all language for God is inadequate, metaphors and models of God are more than purely human projections but not the only appropriate, true ones. As such "metaphors and models of God are understood to be discovered as well as created, to

18. *She Who Is* 12.

relate to God's reality not in the sense of being literally in corre-
spondence with it, but as versions or hypotheses of it that the community accepts as relatively adequate."[19]

Within the context of a metaphoric, constructive theology language serves the purpose of "remythologizing" Christian faith. Its
task is to address the issues that are current for the day. Thus to remythologize for our time means "identifying and elucidating primary metaphors and models from contemporary experience which
will express Christian faith for our day in powerful, illuminating
ways."[20] It is not enough to interpret metaphors and models as they
appear in Scripture and tradition. Instead, the theologian must search
in contemporary life "for images more appropriate to the expression
of Christian faith in our time."[21]

But why metaphors? It is the nature of metaphor that provides a
clue to the answer to this question and to why McFague sees metaphor as the most appropriate image for doing theology. A metaphor
has the character of "is" and "is not." The creative tension that is
caused by bringing together what belongs properly in one context
into use within another enables the theologian to say something
fresh, something altogether new. The dissonance that results sparks
the imagination and generates a moment of discovery. The heuristic
dimension of metaphor has the strongest appeal for McFague. Focus
on discovery prevents the use of metaphors that are dead from
overuse or irrelevance.

When the metaphor gains enough stability and scope to present
a coherent pattern or thought, it becomes a model. A good model
must meet several criteria: "it will be illuminating, fruitful, have relatively comprehensive explanatory ability, be relatively consistent, be
able to deal with anomalies, and so on."[22]

For Johnson "words are pointers."[23] This notion is best understood by examining her use and understanding of analogy. In a return
to the classical sense of analogy with its threefold movement from

---

19. "Imaging a Theology of Nature: The World as God's Body," in Charles
Birch, William Eakin, and Jay McDaniel, eds., *Liberating Life: Contemporary Approaches to Ecological Theology* (Maryknoll, N.Y.: Orbis, 1990) 201–227, at 208.
20. *Models of God* 32.
21. *Models of God* 33.
22. "Imaging a Theology of Nature," 208.
23. *She Who Is* 114.

affirmation to negation to eminence, Johnson focuses on a dynamic of relational knowing, or relational participation. By this she means that "all creatures participate to some degree in 'being,' the very dynamism of existing which God in essence is."[24] To put it simply, she affirms that knowing God is "accomplished in a judgment of the human spirit that affirms God to be inconceivable while at the same time intuiting that the perspective opened up by the intelligible contents of a concept gives a view of God that is trustworthy."[25] The building blocks for this analogous language are creaturely experiences, relationships, qualities, names, and functions. The foundation for analogical predication is a particular interpretation of creation that understands that all things are brought into being and sustained by God. Thus every creature that exists does so through the mystery of divine "being"; as a result of this ontology of participation "every creature in some way shares in divine perfection."[26] It becomes possible to speak of God using the images that arise from creaturely characteristics provided that it is done with the sense that the reality of whom we speak can never be contained in the language. Johnson puts it eloquently: "God is darkly surmised while remaining in essence conceptually inapprehensible."[27]

God is essentially incomprehensible; all language about God is analogical. The use of analogy in theology results in a proliferation of names for God providing a variety of different perspectives that ultimately contribute to an accumulation of wisdom regarding our understanding of who God is while maintaining that the essence of God remains unknowable.

---

24. Ibid.

25. Ibid.

26. *She Who Is* 114. For a full development of the use of analogy in theology see James Francis Anderson, *Reflection on the Analogy of Being* (The Hague: Nijhoff, 1967); David Burrell, *Analogy and Philosophical Language* (New Haven: Yale University Press, 1973), and idem, *Exercises in Religious Understanding* (Notre Dame: University of Notre Dame Press, 1974), especially 80–141 on the language of Thomas Aquinas; Werner Jeanrond and Jennifer L. Rife, eds., *Radical Pluralism and Truth: David Tracy and the Hermeneutics of Religion* (New York: Crossroad, 1991); Janet Martin Soskice, *Metaphor and Religious Language* (New York: Oxford University Press, 1985).

27. *She Who Is* 114.

Assessment

Both McFague and Johnson are very careful to state explicitly the way in which language is used and understood within their theological work. This is to their credit, for it is a substantial dimension in the development of systematic thought. The language of metaphor wields a great deal of power in a heuristic constructivist theology. Its power lies in its ability to shock and thus to stimulate new creative thinking. The "is" and "is not" character of metaphor works as effectively as a compelling parable to "hook" the reader or listener, consequently "jerking" the individual or community out of its complacency. Like a bolt of lightning followed by a clap of thunder, the metaphor exposes the reader or listener to a sudden bright light and startles them with the boldness and noise of a new idea or way of thinking. Old images and symbols are shattered in the experience to make way for fresh ideas. A person's whole system of belief is then reassessed in light of this new image. The best example might be the first time a person considers the female dimension of God or hears God referred to as she. It can be shocking!

But is metaphor enough? The very real dangers that McFague associates with metaphor—irrelevancy and idolatry—can be perceived as the weakness in this system of metaphorical, constructivist theology. First of all, there is a tendency in speech to overuse a new idea or concept. The result is that new and stimulating ideas swiftly become worn out and commonplace. The original "is" and "is not" character of the metaphor is soon forgotten as the metaphor is assimilated into common usage. The metaphor itself becomes literalized and loses its relevance. If death does not occur in the form of irrelevance, it goes the way of idolatry. The metaphor is reified within the tradition and its potency is lost forever. This is not the case, however, with a proper understanding of analogy.

As long as language for God is considered to be analogous there is no danger of irrelevance or idolatry. In contrast to metaphor, analogy provides a wealth of accumulated wisdom in relational terms for a dynamic theology that at once offers insight into God and into creation as a whole while at all times maintaining the ineffability of God.

Authentic analogous language is governed by the threefold pattern of affirmation, negation, and eminence. This pattern assures that the analogy will never become literalized, for the moment of negation sheds a critical light on every image used to gain knowledge of the divine. In the same way the danger of idolatry is also moot, for a clear sense of the ultimate incomprehensibility is consistently maintained. The analogical nature of religious language ensures a plethora of images for divinity and an accumulated wisdom that emerges from biblical, traditional, and contemporary analogies. In this way language for God is timeless, for no matter when it developed or in what circumstance, there is insight to be gained into the mystery of the divine, while the veil of God's aseity remains in place.

The use of analogy has a long history in Christian thought. The Catholic affirmation of the "analogy of being" *(analogia entis)* maintains that it is legitimate to use human concepts and human language to speak about God because of the permanent analogy existing between God's being and all created being. Thus analogy of being is rooted in God's act of creation (and provides the basis for the development of a natural theology). The Catholic position sees no conflict between the analogy of being and the analogy of faith. Rather, according to the doctrine of grace and nature grace does not destroy analogy but, by raising it into analogy of faith, fulfills it. The Protestant "analogy of faith" *(analogia fidei)*, which can be traced to the work of Karl Barth, condemns any such use of the analogy of being because after the Fall there was no longer an analogy of being between God and human beings. Barth's position is based on his insistence that we have a language of theology that comes from revelation in which God and not humanity gives meaning to the words. Barth greatly feared that philosophy (represented by analogy of being) would sit in judgment on the Word of God. Therefore, human words can never of themselves be properly predicated of God. They can express divine reality either by a purely extrinsic attribution, or dialectically, or symbolically, or mythically, or by divine choice.

Returning to the question of McFague's and Johnson's distinctive uses of metaphor and analogy, we note that clearly every use of analogy is metaphorical in the linguistic sense, so one might argue for a limited relationship between them. However, the deeper issues of analogy of being and analogy of faith must be considered when assessing the relationship between metaphor and analogy as they are used in the work of McFague and Johnson. McFague's position on metaphor is grounded in her constructivist methodology. For McFague, metaphors for God are created in the human imagination. This position disallows both analogy of being and analogy of faith, both of which are deeply connected to the community of faith and rooted in a tradition that recognizes and reverences revelation. Her position is in particular disagreement with the Protestant perspective, for it contradicts the essential core of the understanding of analogy based on divine revelation. Thus it can be concluded that McFague does not intend the understanding associated traditionally with analogy when she employs the term metaphor. Instead she uses metaphor in the linguistic sense, as it has been described previously.

On the other hand, when Johnson makes use of analogy in her theology it is apparent that she intends to designate the way in which humanity and all creation share in God's being while remaining cognizant of the fact that as finite humans we can never be one in being with God. Analogy designates relationship. Provided that the threefold method of analogy is used, it facilitates a deeper understanding of the nature of God.

Christological Ramifications

Sallie McFague's constructivist methodology and emphasis on the centrality of metaphor in the use of religious language result in a theocentric christology. In the evolution of her methodology from hermeneutic to heuristic construction McFague has turned away from the accumulated wisdom of the biblical witness and history of Christian tradition. In its place she has opted for the construction of new symbols and images. The one constant in her theological evolution is God. Following her own methodological process, she has constructed a new metaphor for God, the world as God's body. This indeed has had a profound effect on the reformulation of her christological position. The question now becomes how this evolving picture, with its very monotheistic stance, looks on examination.

McFague focuses her attention on the common creation story. In the context of this story she suggests the metaphor of the world as God's body. This metaphor is meant as a replacement for the monarchial image of God that comes from the Scriptures. McFague proposes an "earthly theological agenda," the purpose of which is "to deconstruct and reconstruct the central symbols of the Jewish and Christian traditions in favor of life and its fulfillment, keeping the liberation of the oppressed, including the earth and all its creatures, in central focus."[28]

The metaphor of the earth as God's body assimilates the images traditionally associated with Jesus Christ. Within the framework of the universe as God's body, God is understood as being itself. This God is not distant, but the one in whom we live and breathe and have our being. McFague associates a physicalism with the image of the world as God's body. She states clearly that "it means thinking of God somehow as physical even as we are."[29] In place of the kingly image of God on a distant throne, the world is God's body. Literally, she proclaims, "the world is the bodily presence, a sacrament of the invisible God."[30]

Once again McFague's radical monotheism is exhibited, for the incarnation, traditionally associated with Jesus Christ, is assimilated by the image of the world as God's body. McFague's notion of the incarnation of God is that of a cosmic incarnation. In her model of the universe as God's body, "divine incarnation is not limited to redemption but is everywhere evident in the bodies that live through the breath of the spirit."[31] The role of Christ recedes.

In a startling twist of the biblical story of salvation McFague goes on to suggest that "the world as God's body, then, may be seen as a way to remythologize the suffering love of the cross of Jesus of Nazareth."[32] How is this possible? In the metaphor of the universe as the self-expression of God, God's incarnation, the notions of vulnerability, shared responsibility, and risk are inevitable. The earth, God's body, suffers at the hands of an uncaring humanity.

McFague proposes that "this view provides the basis for a revived sacramentalism—that is a perception of the divine as visible and palpably present."[33] Thus the sacramentalism of the Eucharist, the visible reality of Christ's presence among us, is assumed into this cosmic, theocentric, constructivist theology.

---

28. "An Earthly Theological Agenda," *The Christian Century* 108 (1991) 12–15, at 13.
29. "The World as God's Body," 672.
30. Ibid.
31. *The Body of God* 148.
32. "The World as God's Body," 672.
33. Ibid.

Elizabeth Johnson's revisionist method and use of religious language with special emphasis on analogy yields a christocentric christology. Rather than viewing the authority of Scripture and the Christian tradition as ineffectual, archaic, or obsolete in this postmodern era, and while desiring to attend to the patriarchal dominance that is apparent within them, Johnson employs a threefold method of deconstruction of the patriarchal images and language, retrieving alternative wisdom from the tradition's neglected resources and reconstructing a vision of Christian faith for the future. The result is a revisioned christology with Christ at its center.

Johnson enlists the wisdom literature in deconstructing the dominant patriarchal images and in her retrieval and reconstructing of an image of Christ that promotes the coequal humanity of women and men. It is Johnson's view that when the wisdom tradition is interpreted by means of a feminist hermeneutic it can "offer a way of speaking about Jesus the Christ that can correct the androcentric bias of traditional christology and shape the community and its engagement with the world in an inclusive, freeing, and relational manner."[34]

Relying on the ability of analogical language to help us to speak of the mystery of God and our redemption in Christ Jesus, Johnson uses the image of wisdom as Sophia, the female personification of wisdom found in the Scriptures. Jesus is thus understood to be the child of Sophia who takes on the role and function of traditional wisdom: artisan of all things in creation, life giver, street preacher, prophet, and agent of redemption.

Assessment

Two important results of McFague's use of a constructive methodology and a focus on metaphor are immediately apparent. First, a constructive method can eliminate the problems that have been engendered by patriarchy. When this is coupled with the awareness that all theological language is metaphorical, the possibilities for developing new and appropriate ways of expressing the relationship between God and the world become endless. Theologians are free to explore and develop the creative element of their discipline. In the

---

34. "Wisdom Was Made Flesh and Pitched Her Tent Among Us," in Maryanne Stevens, ed., *Reconstructing the Christ Symbol: Essays in Feminist Christology* (New York: Paulist, 1993) 95–117, at 96.

use of this creative dimension in doing theology, discovery and growth are the vanguards of our evolving understanding of God, humanity, and the world.

Second, McFague's organic model of the world as God's body addresses the ecological concerns of today. She sees this organic model of embodiment as her special contribution because it is "a model that unites us to everything else on our planet in relationships of interdependence."[35] It places theologians in a position within which it is impossible to continue to ignore the androcentric domination of all life and the intrinsic hierarchy that is imposed on the "lower" species.

This method and use of religious language is not without its problems, however. In this constructive view the accumulated wisdom of the Scriptures and Christian tradition is too easily discarded or replaced. Granting that there is a need for critical analysis of symbols, images, and traditions that have lost their meaning through literalization or overuse, granting also that many of these same images have been used as a means of oppression or domination, to assume that there is no wisdom to be gained through a redemption of these symbols is to deny the grace and inspiration of the Spirit in the lives of those who have gone before us. The cost is too great.

Johnson has succeeded in finding a way to address the problems inherent in a patriarchally dominated tradition without losing sight of the wisdom that is contained within it. At the same time she has found a way to revision the tradition that is faithful to inherited truth while responding in faith to the questions and more recent concerns of believers. She accomplishes this task through a careful retrieval of the neglected traditions, most especially the wisdom writings.

35. *The Body of God*, x.

Chapter Six

Constructivist and Revisionist Feminist Christology

"Reclaiming the original inclusive intent of the christological dogma, feminist theology calls the whole church to conversion, away from sexism and toward a community of the discipleship of equals, for the sake of its mission in the world." [1]

Incarnation

The World as God's Body—Sallie McFague

"Christianity is the religion of the incarnation, *par excellence*." [2] With these words McFague situates the incarnation at the center of Christian theology in order to demonstrate the role and significance of embodiment in Christianity. She constructs her argument in defense of the true nature of embodiment and identifies its distortion and ultimate demise at the hands of patriarchy.

The meaning of incarnation (from the Latin for becoming flesh) in Christian doctrine is that the human nature of Jesus Christ was assumed by the divine Word, the *logos,* in a hypostatic union. Jesus Christ is really and truly a human being with everything this implies. [3]

In the context of her metaphor of the world as God's body, McFague suggests that "the primary belief of the Christian commu-

---

1. Johnson, "Redeeming the Name of Christ: Christology," in Catherine Mowry LaCugna, ed., *Freeing Theology: The Essentials of Theology in Feminist Perspective* (San Francisco: Harper Collins, 1993) 115–137, at 134.

2. *Body of God* 14.

3. For comments on McFague's use of incarnation see Ray S. Anderson, "The Incarnation of God in Feminist Christology," in Alvin F. Kimel, ed., *Speaking the*

nity, its doctrine of the incarnation (the belief that God is with us here on earth), be radicalized beyond Jesus of Nazareth to include all matter."[4] Body becomes the primary focus for McFague's ecological theology. Here she speaks not only of the human body but of the body of the earth, which is but a tiny cell in the body of the universe. McFague extends the notion of body to include not only living forms, humans, animals, and plants, but all matter in the universe. Applying the metaphor of body to inanimate objects as well as to living things confirms the material base of all that exists: "body is a model that links us with everything in the most intimate way."[5]

In relation to the organic model she has proposed McFague places the agential model, thereby completing the image of the world as God's body. The organic model alone leads to pantheism, the belief that "the world is, becomes, divine."[6] In the agential model God is assumed to be an agent whose intentions and purposes are realized in history. In her rendering of this model McFague elects to understand spirit, the breath of God, as the agential form God takes. In this way transcendence and immanence are preserved. God is related to the world as spirit is to body. The result is panentheistic: "God is not exhausted by finite beings, not even all finite beings, yet God is *in* all finite creatures and apart from God there is nothing; nor is God 'apart' from anything."[7] The world as God's body is sustained by the breath of the spirit that enlivens it. This dependence on the sustaining breath of God includes *all* of life. Thus McFague concludes that the purpose of creation is not exclusively human beings but "the fecundity, richness, and diversity of *all* that is bodied forth from God and sustained in life by the breath of God."[8] A cosmological christology emerges from this model, which radicalizes the incarnation beyond Jesus of Nazareth to include all matter.

McFague is extremely critical of what she calls the scandal of uniqueness, which claims that God is embodied in one place and

---

Christian God: The Holy Trinity and the Challenge of Feminism (Grand Rapids: Eerdmans, 1992) 288–312.

4. *Body of God*, xi.
5. *Body of God* 17.
6. *Body of God* 140.
7. Raymond Keith Williamson, *Introduction to Hegel's Philosophy of Religion* (Albany, N.Y.: SUNY Press, 1984) 254, quoted by McFague, *Body of God* 149.
8. *Body of God* 148.

only in one way, in the person of Jesus of Nazareth. She finds it absurd and offensive to consider that Jesus alone is the "image of the invisible God" (Col. 1:15). In her view this vision is too limited, for it restricts the divine presence to the thirty-year span of one human being's life on this planet. Given the extent of what is now known about the universe McFague finds it implausible to consider constraining the image of the invisible God to one man. She also sees this narrow vision of incarnation as an affront to other world religions. She makes the bold claim that "God is not present to us in just one place (Jesus of Nazareth, although and especially, paradigmatically there), but in and through all bodies, the bodies of the sun and moon, trees and rivers, animals and people."[9]

McFague believes that Christian faith at its heart is a claim that the universe is on the side of life and its fulfillment. In addition the Christian believes that "we have some clues for fleshing out this claim in the life, death, and appearances of Jesus of Nazareth."[10] Rather than focusing her understanding of the incarnation on the uniqueness of the Christian claim regarding Jesus Christ she highlights instead two critical motifs of the christological tradition understood within the context of the embodiment model: "became flesh" and "lived among us." Ultimately two things matter, "the concrete, physical availability of God's presence and the likeness to ourselves."[11] Thus McFague asserts that one can come to understand the shape and scope of the world as God's body through the christic paradigm.[12] She uses the christic paradigm as a prism or a lens through which to view the metaphor of the universe as God's body. The story of Jesus gives shape to the body. This shape is not a description but a construction that provides the purpose for creation. If we view the universe from the perspective of the paradigmatic story

9. *Body of God* 133.
10. "Imaging a Theology of Nature," in Charles Birch, William Eakin, and Jay McDaniel, eds., *Liberating Life: Contemporary Approaches to Ecological Theology* (Maryknoll, N.Y.: Orbis, 1990) 201–227, at 204.
11. *Body of God* 160.
12. McFague uses "paradigm" interchangeably with "model." A model is understood to be a metaphor with "staying power." "A model is a metaphor that has gained sufficient stability and scope so as to present a pattern for relatively comprehensive and coherent explanation" (*Models of God* 34).

of Jesus, the goal and direction of creation is "toward inclusive love for all, especially the oppressed, the outcast, and the vulnerable."[13]

The narrative of Jesus' life, God as Lover, is a resource for a theology that seeks to liberate. The power of the story, in McFague's theological critique, is recognized in its threefold "destabilizing, inclusive, nonhierarchical vision."[14] It is this vision that leads to an understanding of salvation.

Sophia Incarnate—Elizabeth A. Johnson

Where McFague invokes the use of a newly constructed metaphor for getting at a radicalized understanding of the incarnation, Johnson returns to the traditions of the ancient Hebrews and to the early Christian community to retrieve an image for addressing the incarnation: Wisdom.

Johnson asserts and proceeds to demonstrate that there is a clear connection between Jesus and the Jewish figure of Wisdom (*hokmah* in Hebrew, *sophia* in Greek). She notes that "what Judaism said of Sophia, Christian hymn-makers and epistle writers came to say of Jesus."[15] The earliest form of Christian wisdom christology as found in Paul did not transgress the bounds of monotheism; however, Paul's reflections on the connection between Jesus and Wisdom focused him in a trinitarian direction. Jesus, a human being, was being identified with divine Sophia, who personified God's gracious activity in the world. Johnson concludes, "Jesus then could not be simply a human being inspired by God, but must be closely associated in a unique way with God."[16] In concert with James D. G. Dunn, Johnson sees this unique association of Jesus and wisdom as "the origin of the doctrine of incarnation."[17]

---

13. *Body of God* 160.

14. *Models of God* 48.

15. "Jesus, the Wisdom of God: A Biblical Basis for Non-androcentric Christology," *EThL* 16 (1985) 261–294, at 261.

16. "Jesus, the Wisdom of God," 278.

17. *Christology in the Making: A New Testament Inquiry into the Origins of the Doctrine of the Incarnation* (Philadelphia: Westminster, 1990) 212. Dunn makes some important clarifications regarding this connection with the doctrine of the incarnation. First he points out that "to recognize the deity of Christ is to recognize that in Christ God manifested himself, his power as Creator, his love as Saviour, in a full and final

This is a significant point in Johnson's overall christological perspective, for she believes that if wisdom is one of the key origins for the doctrine of the incarnation, then "whoever espouses a wisdom Christology is asserting that Jesus is the human being Sophia became."[18] The added benefit for Johnson is that Sophia has been traditionally personified as a female. Thus to make the link between Jesus and Sophia is "to confess Jesus the Christ as the incarnation of God imaged in female symbol."[19]

Jesus is Sophia incarnate. By this unqualified statement Johnson intends that Jesus be understood as sharing an intimate solidarity with the unoriginate God and an equally intimate solidarity with humanity. Jesus embodies the divine characteristics of Sophia: creative agency, providential power to order the universe, redeeming agency, prophecy; quite literally, wisdom is simply God.[20]

Johnson attributes the insight into Jesus' ontological relationship with God to the early Christian community's use of the wisdom categories. As a consequence of New Testament sapiential christology "Jesus came to be seen as God's only-begotten Son."[21]

Assessment: Conversation

It is immediately apparent that McFague and Johnson differ widely on their understanding of incarnation. McFague hopes to radicalize the Christian notion of incarnation. Proceeding from the theocentric vision that has guided her theology from the start, she enlarges the concept of incarnation such that "becoming flesh" indicates the metaphor of the world as God's body rather than an individual divine/human embodiment. Incarnation is the primary exemplar of McFague's theology, for embodiment is the focus of her organic-

---

way." Second, he is careful to note that "when one says that divine wisdom became incarnate in Christ, that means that Christ was the climactic and definitive embodiment of God's own creative power and saving concern."

18. *She Who Is* 99.

19. Ibid.

20. For a further delineation of the characteristics ascribed to wisdom see Johnson, "Wisdom Was Made Flesh and Pitched Her Tent Among Us," in Maryanne Stevens, ed., *Reconstructing the Christ Symbol: Essays in Feminist Christology* (New York: Paulist, 1993) 95–117, at 100–102.

21. "Wisdom Was Made Flesh," 106.

agential model. However, within this model the role of Jesus Christ is relativized, for he is seen as only one among many incarnations of God in the world. McFague will go so far as to name Jesus the foundational figure for Christianity, but his uniqueness ends there. Jesus is no more divine and no less divine than any other person who attempts to live in loving mutual relationship with God. She identifies several "incarnations of divine love: John Woolman, Sojourner Truth, Dietrich Bonhoeffer, Dorothy Day, Martin Luther King, Jr., to name a few of the better-known disciples."[22]

Jesus is viewed as Christianity's historical choice as the premier paradigm of God's love. McFague argues further that Jesus is "not ontologically different from other paradigmatic figures either in our tradition or in other religious traditions who manifest in word and deed the love of God for the world."[23] In this matter McFague's position is markedly different from Johnson's, and I would suggest from the commonly accepted understanding of the Christian tradition.

To remove Jesus as the central figure from Christianity is to dilute Christian tradition to the point of dissolution. Placing Jesus Christ at the center of the tradition is the distinguishing mark of the Christian faith. In her desire to rid the tradition of exclusive imagery, especially male-dominated symbols that ignore or devalue the role of women, McFague has thrown out the proverbial "baby with the bath water." Rather then looking to the tradition to find ways in which the image of Jesus Christ can be redeemed in favor of the coequal humanity of women, McFague disarms the ontological significance of the human Jesus by completely relativizing his person and function. The result is that the transcendent reality of God has been rejected in favor of God's immanence. The significance of God's enduring gift of Jesus who became truly one of us while remaining one with God is superseded by the incarnation of the world as God's body. What is losing ground here is the relationship between the identity of Christianity that has been handed down and shared by the community of believers and the need for relevance in today's world. In McFague's attempt to be utterly relevant through the construction of metaphors and models for God that respond to contemporary needs, Christian identity has been sacrificed.

22. *Models of God* 136.
23. Ibid.

Johnson, on the other hand, has successfully maintained the relationship between classical Christian identity and postmodern concerns by reexamining the Scriptures and tradition in search of forgotten images and analogies that meet both needs. Her understanding of incarnation, which links Jesus with Sophia, personified wisdom, addresses the concerns of exclusivity while maintaining a christocentric perspective.

Both transcendence and immanence are provided for in the image of Jesus-Sophia. In Johnson's own words, "female Sophia represents creative transcendence, primordial passion for justice, and knowledge of the truth while Jesus incarnates these divine characteristics in an immanent way relative to bodiliness and the earth."[24] This rearticulation of a core Christian symbol is successful in subverting the male-dominated images of the tradition while remaining faithful to the accumulated wisdom of the community of faith.

Johnson and McFague focus our attention on the cherished feminist value of embodiment. Rejecting the sharp dichotomy of body and spirit traditionally espoused by Christianity, they return to the ancient wisdom that graciously received and recognized the gift of God's intimate presence in the universe. While McFague repudiates the claim that God is uniquely embodied only in Jesus of Nazareth, she highlights the significance of embodiment in the metaphor of the world as God's body. God's presence is made physically available to us and that embodiment in the christic paradigm is a likeness to ourselves. Johnson celebrates the embodiment of God in human flesh, for the mystery of God is opened to all it means to be human. God is irreversibly, physically linked to the human adventure. Humanity is sacramentalized in a mutual relationship with God for all time.

Salvation

Creation-Centered Salvation—Sallie McFague

McFague's methodology of construction and use of metaphor has a profound effect on her understanding of salvation. McFague seeks to expand the vision of salvation through her use of the meta-

24. *She Who Is* 165.

phor of the world as God's body. In a move intended to overcome the dualistic split of spirit and body which has been so much a part of classic theology, McFague attempts to demonstrate that salvation ought to be as concerned for "such basic needs as food, clothing and shelter"[25] as it has been for matters of the spirit and eternity.

McFague's first step is to make a clear distinction between the terms redemption and salvation. Redemption means to "buy back" or to "repay." In the tradition this repayment demands great sacrifice; moreover, its application is limited to human beings. Specifically, McFague notes, this redemption implies that it is human beings "who have offended (sinned) and hence need to be rescued through a substitutionary act of reconciliation."[26]

On the other hand, salvation connotes healing or preserving from destruction. When this is considered in light of the metaphor of the world as God's body the result is an understanding of salvation that involves the well-being of the natural order that, along with human beings, needs to be healed and preserved. Using a healing metaphor for salvation suggests preservation from destruction and restoration to health and adequate bodily function. Salvation is thus oriented to the here and now. It is associated with what is physical. In the organic model the world is seen through the eyes of the body. As a result, McFague insists, "we can never again think of salvation in spiritual, otherworldly, atemporal, or nonspatial ways."[27]

Having distinguished between redemption and salvation, and keeping to the modest claim that salvation can be understood in terms of a healing metaphor, McFague focuses on the need for salvation. The need, she claims, arises from the suffering of creation. Perhaps the best way to deal with what McFague means by the need for salvation is to explore "saving" as the activity she associates with God as lover in her model of God for an ecological and nuclear age. In this context McFague outlines her understanding of salvation and compares it to the classic Christian model. Salvation can only be understood in light of McFague's organic model, which focuses on God as lover of the whole world in all of its immensity, complexity,

25. "The World as God's Body," *The Christian Century* 105 (1988) 671–673, at 672.

26. *Models of God* 168.

27. *Body of God* 200.

and intricacy. In this model salvation must "take into account the organic solidarity of our actual situation."[28]

The consequence of this is a realization that the model has a tragic side. First of all, the evolutionary process itself dictates that some species will be sacrificed for the sake of the perpetuation and evolution of others. This is a part of the experience in which we find ourselves and there is little alternative to consenting to the situation as it exists. A second, more disturbing consequence is realized in the threat of nuclear annihilation, for it brings us face to face with a deepening of the situation in which human sin occurs. McFague interprets the nuclear threat as the ultimate temptation "to be like God not merely by knowing good and evil but by exercising ultimate power over good and evil."[29] In this way the nuclear threat symbolizes the ultimate sin, for within this model

> sin is the turning-away not from a transcendent power but from interdependence with all other beings, including the matrix of being from whom all life comes. It is not pride or unbelief but the refusal of relationship—the refusal to be the beloved of our lover God and the refusal to be lover of all God loves.[30]

Understood in this way, sin disrupts the balance of life. A desire for union with everything else becomes a desire for the self alone. When this self-love becomes the focus, the balance of radical interdependence is disrupted and life itself is threatened. In the end McFague ascribes sin to human selfishness and the result is estrangement and alienation. Consequently hierarchies, dualisms, and outcasts become the norm.

This conception of sin within the model of the world as God's body, in which God is lover, begs the question of God's role in the evil that is part of this evolutionary process. McFague's theodicy states quite simply, "God as lover suffers with those who suffer."[31] McFague uses the example of the Jewish Holocaust to clarify what she means. "God was not in the Nazi death camps, but they are in God."[32] The gift, then, is God's presence, for we never suffer alone.

28. *Models of God* 138.
29. Ibid.
30. *Models of God* 139.
31. *Models of God* 142.
32. Ibid.

McFague, however, sees this passion of God as the last stance toward sin, the first being resistance, understood as an active effort to heal. Salvation is achieved in a vastly different way in this model than it has been in the reigning classic model of Jesus Christ. It differs primarily in terms of "*who* brings it about, *what* its nature is, and *how* it is received."[33]

Who Brings About Salvation?

In the classic model the *who* is Jesus Christ. As representative of us all, he brings about salvation through his life, death, and resurrection. In the ecological evolutionary view, the *who* is all of us. With God we are all involved in the ongoing healing of the body of God. Thus salvation itself is ongoing and the responsibility of all people. McFague allows for paradigmatic manifestations of God's love, such as Jesus was and is for Christians, but she is very clear in stating that "the kind of solidarity implicit in the model of God as lover in an ecological, evolutionary context does not allow the work of one individual to be effective for all space and time."[34]

What Is the Nature of Salvation?

The *what* of salvation also differs from the classic model. Traditionally the presupposition of the doctrine of salvation is that atonement is made for sins. McFague sees this as a stress on the negative aspect of salvation, for the focus is on what has gone wrong. In her model the work of salvation is first the illumination that all of us are loved by God. This announcement is made to the beloved, who is not an individual human being but the world. The second movement is the response of the beloved to the message of love. Those who hear the message are "energized to work to overcome alienation, to heal wounds, to include the outcasts."[35] What becomes apparent here is that McFague has singled out one classic model and fails to emphasize or attend to the plurality of images, metaphors, and models that have been utilized in the tradition.

---

33. *Models of God* 143.
34. Ibid.
35. *Models of God* 144.

How Is Salvation Received?

Finally, the question of *how* salvation is received or made effective must be examined. McFague points out that in classical theology "salvation is available through the preached word and the sacraments."[36] She perceives it to be a form of passive acceptance of an action (taking away of sin) that took place two thousand years ago. This view is not persuasive, for it does not involve the present work of all the beloved laboring along with the lover to relieve the pain of alienation.

The *how* of McFague's model involves action. The love extended by God as lover calls for a response, and the only response possible is love. In McFague's picture of salvation all of us are active participants; we participate in the process of making whole. In McFague's view salvation requires action on our part. We are saved to the degree that we work and love the whole world. McFague sums up what is required:

> What is needed on this view of salvation is not the forgiveness of sins so that the elect may achieve their reward, but a *metanoia*—a conversion or change of sensibility, a new orientation at the deepest level of our being—from one concerned with our own salvation apart from the world to one directed toward the well-being, the health, of the whole body of the world. Salvation, then, is not a "second work" of God; it belongs intrinsically to the "first work," creation. Salvation is a deepening of creation: it says to all, even to the last and the least, not only, "It is good that you exist!" but also, "You are valuable beyond all knowing, all imagining." The saviors of the world are lovers of the world.[37]

In the model of the world as God's body, in which the shape of God's body is determined by the christic paradigm, the need is addressed by the scope of the body, which is the cosmic Christ, understood to be "the loving, compassionate God on the side of those who suffer, especially the vulnerable and excluded."[38] In this way whatever happens to us, the world, happens to God as well. This cosmic Christ is the resurrected Christ, freed from the body of Jesus of Nazareth and thus present in all bodies.

36. *Models of God* 145.
37. *Models of God* 146.
38. *Body of God* 179.

The distinctive feature of McFague's understanding of salvation is an emphasis on place and space as opposed to the traditional focus on a temporal mode. In her view Christian tradition has seen salvation in terms of time, "the beginning in creation; the middle in the incarnation, ministry, and death of Jesus Christ; and the end at the eschaton when God shall bring about the fulfillment of all things."[39] This new emphasis emerges from a concern for where God's body is present in its christic shape. Specifically it arises from an ecological sensibility that in McFague's view necessitates that we broaden the circle of salvation to include the natural world, and the practical issues that will face us will, more and more, be ones of space, not time.

McFague contends that "salvation is the *direction* of creation and creation is the *place* of salvation."[40] Interestingly, McFague regards this position as a statement of faith. It must be a faith stance, she claims, because it is only understood retrospectively. From the standpoint of the life and ministry of Jesus, which is signified by healing, table fellowship, and divine liberation, one looks back at the progression of creation and projects the notion of salvation onto the entire evolutionary pattern. It is necessary to read back into creation the hope that all of creation experiences divine liberation, healing, and inclusive love. From a Christian perspective the entirety of creation is understood to be the cosmic Christ, the body of God in the christic paradigm. McFague concludes, "the direction or hope of creation, all of it, is nothing less than what I understand that paradigm to be for myself and for other human beings: the liberating, healing, inclusive love of God."[41]

The second element of this dimension of the cosmic Christ involves place. Creation is the place of salvation. From this perspective salvation is concerned with the "here-and-now aspect of spatiality."[42] This translates into an understanding of salvation as happening now and available to the needy outcast in creation. Creation is not perceived as the backdrop of salvation, but instead becomes of central importance, for salvation takes place within creation and involves all of creation. This agential, organic model of the world as God's body,

39. *Body of God* 180.
40. Ibid.
41. *Body of God* 181.
42. Ibid.

shaped by the christic paradigm and extended to the dimension of the cosmic Christ, literally embodies salvation.

Jesus, the Concrete Foundation of Salvation—Elizabeth A. Johnson

In an address to the members of the Catholic Theological Society of America Johnson considered the question of how, in the light of historical consciousness, we are to understand Jesus as the concrete foundation of salvation coming from God through the power of the Holy Spirit. She identified two ways in which this historical consciousness has had an impact on the doctrine of soteriology. First, "it heightens awareness of the contextual nature of events, so that even the events of 'salvation history' are now seen to be the result of intramundane causality."[43] Consequently the interpretation of texts is altered by what can be discerned of the probable historical events at their origin. Second, "historical consciousness underscores the contingency of real history."[44] The result is that the traditional doctrine of Christian soteriology must deal with the "radically contingent historical nature of events."[45]

Johnson examined Jesus and salvation within the framework of historical consciousness from three perspectives: past—how it has reshaped the reading of Scripture and tradition about salvation; present—an assessment of contemporary formulations; and future—a look at the issues that provide the agenda for ongoing work.

Past: Reshaping the Reading of Scripture and Tradition

A review of historical studies shows that the language of Scripture is narrative and metaphoric. The stories and images originate in lived experiences, actual encounters between Jesus and the men and women who were a part of his life. These events took place in a variety of historical contexts. The encounters had an impact on history as they came to be narrated by the early Christian community. Consequently the metaphors and images associated with salvation were plentiful and varied. Johnson points out that "the word salvation itself is one of these metaphors which in both its Hebrew and Greek

---

43. "Jesus and Salvation," in Paul Crowley, ed., CTSA *Proceedings* 49 (1994) 2.
44. Ibid.
45. *Body of God* 3.

forms connotes being rescued, snatched away from peril as well as being healed or preserved in well-being."[46] Recognizing the existence of a plethora of interpretations of Scripture[47] that have resulted from this historical consciousness, Johnson retrieves the often neglected tradition of wisdom literature to revision an understanding of salvation that has been ignored or forgotten in tradition.[48]

Johnson equates the characteristics and roles of Jesus with divine Sophia. The incarnation of Jesus is the embodiment of Sophia herself in the world. She concludes that "the saving significance of Jesus (functional christology, Christ *pro nobis*) can be understood in wisdom categories."[49] Wisdom appears in Job and Proverbs; she is active in Sirach, Baruch, and the Wisdom of Solomon; she even shows up in the intertestamental literature such as Enoch. The portrait that emerges is multifaceted. In fact, there has been a great deal of scholarly debate about how all the various images of Sophia might be interpreted or combined to create a portrait that mirrors her significance in the life and beliefs of the people of Israel.

In Johnson's judgment the interpretation that bears the most fruit in christology is Sophia as "the personification of God's own self coming toward the world, dwelling in it, active for its well-being."[50] It is here that Sophia's saving actions are most apparent. Significant among the attributes of wisdom is her redeeming agency. Throughout history human beings were "saved by wisdom" (Wis 9:18). In the Wisdom of Solomon a series of examples appear that point to Sophia's saving action, both delivering and preserving humankind. Johnson points out that in the Christian Scriptures the use of wisdom categories to interpret Jesus "deepened their understanding of his saving deeds by placing them in continuity with Wisdom's saving work throughout history."[51]

In much the same way that many biblical interpretations of salvation exist, so too in the post-biblical tradition a "vigor of interpretations of salvation in differing historical contexts continued

46. *Body of God* 4.

47. Johnson points out such categories for salvation as financial, legal, cultic, political, personal, medical, existential, and familial.

48. Johnson's acknowledgement of the plurality of interpretations is in stark contrast to McFague's focus on one classic model.

49. "Jesus, the Wisdom of God," 291.

50. "Wisdom Was Made Flesh," 99.

51. "Wisdom Was Made Flesh," 105.

unabated."[52] In the early centuries there emerged Irenaeus' recapitulation theory and Athanasius' divinization theology in the East, Tertullian's satisfaction theory and Augustine's sacrificial theory in the West. In the eleventh century these interpretations began to recede in the West as a result of Anselm's restructuring of the satisfaction theory. Simply stated, this theory proposed that God became a human being and died on the cross to take on what was due the honor of God, which had been offended by humanity's sin. This theory has been criticized particularly for its negativity and for its fostering of the notion of an angry God. In current theology Johnson sees a growing consensus that "theology today needs to interpret Jesus as the concrete foundation of salvation in ways other than the primarily juridical and cultic notions that have accrued around this theory."[53]

Present: Contemporary Formulations

Johnson maintains that "Christian soteriology has basically a narrative structure."[54] The construction is based on the foundational narrative of Jesus as the bringer of salvation. She makes the assessment that current work in soteriology takes the form of three types of foundational narrative. In examining these positions Johnson is careful to point out that "typologies are never completely adequate to the reality they seek to model."[55]

The first type is what Johnson calls the mythical narrative, which is a product of pre-modern thought processes devoid of historical consciousness. It takes place outside of time and features the interpretation of prototypical events within archetypal patterns. In this age of historical consciousness this form of narrative is difficult to maintain.

The second form of foundational narrative identified by Johnson is the totalizing historical narrative. This type has two critical components. First, it is expressive of the modern mentality, which is historical, and second, it is totalizing in that it is characterized by modernity's optimistic and universalizing tendencies. The focus of this narrative form is the intelligible interpretation of all history, which is given the appearance of a well-ordered emergent structure.

52. "Jesus and Salvation," 4.
53. "Jesus and Salvation," 6.
54. Ibid.
55. "Jesus and Salvation," 7.

Johnson cites Karl Rahner's soteriological position as the best example of the use of the totalizing historical narrative.

> His contribution lies, I think, in the way that he interprets Jesus and
> salvation through the skillful interplay of transcendental and categor-
> ical moments, so that the link between the gracious mystery of God,
> Jesus' historical life, and salvation for all becomes intelligible in a
> modern, historically conscious framework of thought.[56]

The third type of narrative may be called contingent historical
narrative.[57] Johnson relates this form of narrative to the postmodern
mentality. Postmodernity, according to Johnson, is "conscious of the
ambiguous character of progress advanced through so much suffering and defeat."[58] Aware of the threatened character of existence and
the vulnerability of the human project, this postmodern disposition
makes use of a historical narrative that incorporates contingency into
its telling.

The contingent historical narrative retells the story of Jesus'
ministry, teaching, suffering, death, and resurrection in such a way
that God's presence is recognized in the midst of historical disconti-
nuities. The story is neither preordained nor predictable; rather, it
happens within the context of historical forces in the same way that
all lives happen. This narrative generates hope, Johnson maintains,
for "it signals divine mystery unpredictably present in the very midst
of contingent events of suffering, community, struggle, joy, present
where least expected, even with the disinherited and brokenhearted,
irrepressible in vitality."[59]

Johnson asks: given that Christian soteriology has narrative
structure at its heart, which of the narrative forms as expressed here
is the most appropriate for defining the status of the theological question in the present? It is apparent that Johnson herself finds the contingent historical narrative form the most appropriate for defining the
question of salvation. Her position is vividly portrayed in her interpretation of the events that led up to the crucifixion and death of

---

56. "Jesus and Salvation," 8.
57. Johnson associates this form of narrative with the work of Johannes Baptist
Metz, Edward Schillebeeckx, and other European theologians as well as liberationist,
feminist theologians and political theologians: "Jesus and Salvation," 9.
58. Ibid.
59. Ibid.

Jesus. Rather than approaching the story from the Anselmian perspective, according to which the form of Jesus' suffering and death was determined by God as repayment for sin, Johnson relates the actions and experiences of Jesus to the actions and experiences of Sophia. Jesus is preeminent in the long line of Sophia's prophets. For Johnson "Jesus' death is a consequence of the hostile response of religious and civil rulers to the style and content of his ministry, to which he was radically faithful with a freedom that would not quit."[60] Jesus' death occurred as a consequence of his fidelity to God.

However, the story does not end here. Spirit-Sophia bestows her characteristic gift of life. Through her power Jesus is raised from the dead and the message and the gift of life do not stop there. Johnson includes the circle of Jesus' disciples in the gift, for "they are missioned to make the inclusive goodness and saving power of Sophia-God experientially available to the ends of the earth."[61]

Understood within the wisdom categories, the story of the cross and resurrection is linked to the ways of Sophia, who seeks justice and peace in a world of domination and violence. After the resurrection the story of Jesus-Sophia shifts from the contingent historical existence of Jesus of Nazareth to the community of believers who are filled with the Spirit. The legacy of the Scriptures and tradition does not stop with the first disciples. Johnson recognizes that "biblical cosmic Christology expands the notion of Christ still further (Col 1:15-20), seeing the universe itself is destined to be christomorphic in a reconciled new heaven and new earth."[62]

Future: Ongoing Work in Soteriology

Johnson charts five areas that outline the current soteriological frontier: God, christology, anthropology, the cross, and world religions. The dialogue taking place regarding these important questions, particularly from the perspective of critical, postmodern, post-Enlightenment narrative, defines the soteriological agenda.

For Johnson the focus is christology. The postmodern move is toward the retrieval of the entire life of Jesus as salvific. Whereas in the past the focus has been almost exclusively on the passion and

60. *She Who Is* 158.
61. Ibid.
62. *She Who Is* 162.

death of Jesus, Johnson notes, "the repair of the world is signaled in his entire life as salvific."[63]

Johnson is also concerned over reinterpretation of the cross. Reconsideration of the reality of the cross from the historical perspective calls into question the traditional satisfaction theory. In its place are new interpretations that understand the cross as the consequence of the faithful life and ministry practiced by Jesus of Nazareth. The result is a shift in our understanding of God from perpetrator to participant in the pain and suffering of the world.

The logical next step for Johnson is consideration of theological post-modernism's relationship to other world religions. At this juncture three well-known positions regarding Jesus and salvation have been identified: exclusivist, inclusivist, and pluralist.[64] The exclusivist response takes the position that our (Christian) community, our tradition, our understanding of reality is the true one, excluding all others. This position leaves no room for dialogue with other world religions. Rahner's notion of the "anonymous Christian" is considered by Johnson and others to be a prime example of the inclusivist position. According to Johnson, "Rahner combines the constitutive sense of Jesus Christ for salvation with the value of other religious traditions which include elements of Christic grace and truth for their historically diverse members."[65] The pluralist response, seen primarily in the work of Paul J. Knitter,[66] in Johnson's words, "affirms a unique and universally relevant manifestation of salvation in Jesus

---

63. "Jesus and Salvation," 11.

64. For further reading regarding these positions see Paul F. Knitter, *No Other Name? A Critical Survey of Christian Attitudes Toward the World Religions*, American Society of Missiology Series 7 (Maryknoll, N.Y.: Orbis, 1985); Paul J. Knitter, ed., *Pluralism and Oppression: Theology in World Perspective*, The Annual Publication of the College Theology Society 24 (New York: University Press of America, 1988); John Hick and Paul F. Knitter, eds., *The Myth of Christian Uniqueness: Toward a Pluralistic Theology of Religions* (Maryknoll, N.Y.: Orbis, 1987); Gavin D'Costa, *Theology and Religious Pluralism: The Challenge of Other Religions* (Oxford: Basil Blackwell, 1986); Gavin D'Costa, ed., *Christian Uniqueness Reconsidered: The Myth of a Pluralistic Theology of Religions*, Faith Meets Faith Series (Maryknoll, N.Y.: Orbis, 1990).

65. "Jesus and Salvation," 16.

66. For an account of Paul J. Knitter's understanding of salvation see his "Christian Salvation: Its Nature and Uniqueness—An Interreligious Proposal," *New Theology Review* 7 (1994) 33–46.

while eschewing its absolute normativity, thus arriving at a non-nor-mative, theocentric Christology."[67]

While Johnson's position gravitates toward the inclusivist framework, she continues to make strides toward an expanding vision of Christian soteriology through revisioning the Christian understanding of Jesus and salvation. Johnson believes that postmodern narrative soteriology provides the most fruitful framework of thought for entering into dialogue and for recognizing that Jesus is the concrete foundation of salvation. In addition, Johnson has an expanded vision of the role of the Spirit. She sees the ongoing work of salvation present in the cosmic Christ who expresses more than the historical Jesus, and who is present and active in human history. Johnson summarizes her position:

> For the concrete Jesus of history is uncreated Wisdom in kenotic form, enfleshed within the contingency of history. The radical *kenosis* of the Incarnation means that even when the Chalcedonian confession is affirmed in all its fullness, the contingent, historical character of the Jesus event allows for the possibility that the divine offer of salvation finds different concrete forms in other contingent contexts. Confessing Jesus the Christ as the universal Savior, Christian belief remains attuned to hear from others in dialogue how God's saving ways have also been active among them.[68]

For Johnson the gracious mystery of God is present in this world offering the strength of resistance in the face of suffering, and the gift of healing and liberation in the midst of the contingency of this world.

Assessment: Conversation

The differences between McFague's and Johnson's soteriological positions are clear. For McFague salvation takes place exclusively within this world. It is the responsibility of human beings in cooperation with God to work for the liberation and well-being of all creation. McFague's is a creation-centered notion of salvation. Salvation has to do with the body, specifically with the world as God's body. On the other hand, Johnson's notion of salvation involves both

---

67. "Jesus and Salvation," 16.
68. Ibid.

the experience of this world and the fullness of life with God in a future eschatological encounter.

In McFague's view salvation is an ongoing evolutionary event in which we are all active participants. Jesus' life and death offer to us a model or paradigm of a life lived in fidelity to God. She states very clearly that salvation cannot be exclusively associated with the events of the life of one man who lived nearly two thousand years ago and whose life lasted for the brief span of thirty years. In stark contrast, Johnson believes that Jesus is the concrete foundation of salvation. Jesus-Sophia embodies the saving love of God. By his life and death Jesus revealed the saving love of God in our midst. Jesus offers the presence of God in the contingency of this earthly life. The cosmic Christ, whose spirit supersedes the earthly Jesus, is present in this world offering universal salvation.

Both Johnson and McFague seek an understanding of salvation that responds to the concerns of liberation of all (not just human beings) who are oppressed, that addresses the ecological crises of the planet, and that restores the biblical notion of universal salvation.

Chapter Seven

Epilogue:
Quilts and Braided Bridges

Proceeding from the belief that christology stands at the heart of the Christian tradition, I have engaged christological questions that address the feminist critique of traditional christology. Sallie McFague and Elizabeth A. Johnson have undertaken the considerable task of critiquing the Christian tradition in response to their own personal questions and broadly in response to the questions of all women who have struggled to find their place and their voice in the Church. McFague's hope was to design a "quilt square" that represented her unique contribution to the contemporary "theological quilt." Johnson attempted to unite classical theology with feminist theology through braiding a footbridge that enabled mutual critque and exchange.

Insights and Reflections

Sallie McFague's constructivist feminist approach to doing theology is courageous and bold. There are striking elements of her methodology and use of religious language that demand attention and offer a theological challenge. The first is her use of metaphor. McFague sees the use of metaphor as central to theology. Declaring all theology to be at its heart metaphorical, she proceeds to carefully analyze traditional metaphors and construct new ones that speak to contemporary concerns. This process of construction is dependent upon truly creative imagination. As a result the theologian is dared to dream, to take up the role of poet, creating new images to replace those that have lost their ability to have an impact on the lives of believers. The responsibility of theologians becomes the construction of new Christian metaphors and models that will address the concerns of the contemporary world, particularly on behalf of all the oppressed members of this planet.

The second challenging aspect of McFague's use of method and language is its constructive dimension. Construction is liberating. It frees theology from its attachment to reified and irrelevant models and images. It opens the door for feminist theologians to engage in the creative task of designing new images and models that speak to the long-neglected experience of women. It frees theology to move beyond an androcentric focus with its inherent hierarchy to a cosmological focus that considers all the elements of this universe significant and worthy of concern. In addition it positively affirms the pluralistic nature of this world, freeing Christian theology to enter into dialogue with other world religions with the hope for new insights and the strengthening of faith.

Along with the challenges of McFague's use of method and religious language come two dangers. The first is apparent in her critical analysis of the Christian tradition. McFague is prepared to discard Christian images and models, whether from the Scripture or from the inherited tradition, in favor of new constructions that respond to contemporary issues.[1] The danger is the loss of past wisdom. The criteria for assessing the traditional models come from the present moment. The notion that revelation has a transcendent quality that enables it to continue to have significance and meaning beyond its historical context is dismissed. The authority of revelation is nullified beyond its historical context. Emphasis is placed upon new creative imaginings that respond to the current need in lieu of traditional wisdom. Too much in the tradition is too easily discarded.

---

1. For a critique of this position see James Moulder, "Why Feminist Theology Encourages Unbelief," in Johan Mouton, Andries van Aarde, and Willem Vorster, eds., *Paradigms and Progress in Theology* (Pretoria: Human Sciences Research Council, 1988) 252–258; Ray C. Penn, "Competing Hermeneutical Foundations and Religious Communication: Why Protestants Can't Understand Each Other," *The Journal of Communication and Religion* 11 (1988) 10–21; Blake K. Richter, "Recent Views of the Revelatory Character of the Bible and Their Implications for Its Interpretation," D.Min. Thesis. San Francisco Theological Seminary, 1993; David Tracy, "Metaphor and Religion: The Test Case of Christian Texts," in Sheldon Sacks, ed., *On Metaphor* (Chicago: University of Chicago Press, 1979) 89–104.

The second danger has been identified by McFague herself. Metaphor is always prone to irrelevance and idolatry. In this sense metaphor is limited in its ability to transmit the transcendent dimensions of Christian faith, particularly regarding the nature of God. In contrast to analogy, which is employed by Johnson, metaphor does not incorporate the threefold pattern of affirmation, negation, and eminence, which protects the image from irrelevance and idolatry.

This brings us to the first significant aspect of Johnson's methodology and use of religious language, her reliance on analogy. Keeping to the longstanding tradition of the use of analogy in theology, Johnson cites it once again as meaningful in the revisioning of Christian tradition in this age. Analogy provides a wealth of accumulated wisdom in relational terms for a dynamic theology that at once offers insight into God and into creation as a whole while at all times maintaining the ineffability of God. The use of analogy prevents the possible lapse into idolatry, for application of the threefold pattern of affirmation, negation, and eminence assures that the analogy will not become literalized. It also avoids the danger of irrelevance by providing an endless number of images and models that are continually assessed for their relevance.

The challenge of this approach to the use of religious language is evident in the consistent application of the threefold pattern that defines the nature of the analogy. Johnson challenges theologians to remember the original nature of analogy as it has been understood within the tradition and to use it to reevaluate the analogical nature of all religious language. Johnson's revisionist approach invites theologians to "look again" at the tradition with a particular focus on attending to neglected and suppressed stories, events, and images that, when surfaced and revisioned in light of today's questions, have the potential to address the current theological issues, especially as they are related to all within the cosmos who have need of liberation. This revisioning allows for the continued contribution of traditional wisdom while critiquing the limitations of the past.

Some might argue that the danger of this method is the external boundary that confines the conversation to the realm of Christianity, creating a kind of "closed-loop" system of evaluation. However, the braiding of the footbridge, which Johnson hopes to accomplish, creates a link to a new conversation partner, feminist theology. If the gulf that separated classical theology and feminist concerns can be spanned, the precedent is established for linkages between Christianity and numerous others. Compared with the potential loss of inherited wisdom that exists in the constructivist method the danger is small.

McFague's christology is paradigmatic and cosmological. For her, Jesus of Nazareth is a paradigmatic figure who for Christians is the most significant model for coming to understand the nature of God. In the evolution of her christology, deeply influenced by the theological work of Gordon D. Kaufman, McFague takes a starkly monotheistic, theocentric perspective. She radicalizes the doctrine of incarnation. In her organic, agential model "becoming flesh" is expanded to mean the world as God's body rather than an individual divine/human embodiment. Within this extended vision the notion of salvation is also amplified. Salvation takes place within the world and all life shares in the responsibility. Human beings, in particular, must work with God to bring about salvation for the entire cosmos. Within this model of the world as God's body, God enters into the experience of suffering. The gift is God's abiding presence, panentheism. For McFague panentheism suggests that "God is embodied but not necessarily totally."[2] In this model God as the spirit is the source, the life, the breath of all reality. She is careful to point out that panentheism remains distinct from both the theist and the pantheist traditions. She borrows her definition from Raymond Keith Williamson: "God is not exhausted by finite beings, not even all finite beings, yet God is *in* all creatures and apart from God there is nothing; nor is God 'apart' from anything."[3]

In McFague's christology, as in her methodology, there are challenges and dangers. McFague challenges theologians to rethink the dualism of body and spirit that is extant in the Christian tradition. Recognizing Christianity as the religion of the body *par excellence* (eucharist, incarnation, mystical body) McFague's embodiment model puts us back in touch with the world in which we live that has been created for us by God. It focuses on the sacredness of the body and its significance beyond this existence. This approach challenges theologians to deal within this earthly realm, to confront the ecological crisis of our age and to expand to a global vision of life.

2. *Body of God* 150.
3. *Introduction to Hegel's Philosophy of Religion* (Albany, N. Y.: SUNY Press, 1984) 254, as quoted in *Body of God* 149.

McFague's understanding of salvation confronts humanity with its role and responsibility regarding the salvation of the entire planet and the seriousness of the sin that neglects or misuses the gifts of the earth. She challenges all of humanity, and theologians in particular, to examine the ramifications of this nuclear age and to respond with new and creative answers to these critical issues.

McFague's christology also extends the dialogue to other world religions. Her position says "yes" to the pluralist agenda that would open up the conversation among religious leaders. She removes one of the greatest stumbling blocks to the exchange when she relativizes the role of Christ.

However, it is this conception of Christ that is problematic. In denying the uniqueness of Christ the Christian message is compromised. Foundationally Jesus Christ is at the center of the tradition, but McFague has reduced the role of Christ both from the standpoint of incarnation and salvation. Jesus is compared to any other significant religious leader, past or present, who can serve as a paradigm for living in right relationship with God. Though willing to acknowledge that Jesus of Nazareth is the premier paradigm of Christianity, McFague is unwilling to ascribe the traditional status of divinity to him. Instead, the significance of God's enduring gift of Jesus who became truly one of us while remaining one with God is superseded by the world, which takes on each significant dimension of the role of Christ: embodiment of the word of God, the revelation and human expression of God, and God's sacramental presence. Quick to fall along with the traditional understanding of Christ is the relevant significance of revelation. This position verges on revolutionary, post-Christian feminism.

Johnson presents a wisdom christology. In a detailed retrieval of the wisdom tradition she relates the life and ministry of Jesus the Christ to the pivotal role of Sophia, the female personification of God's holy wisdom.[4] Johnson challenges theologians to examine the

---

4. In treating the approach to tradition Johnson advocates a positive relationship to the Hebrew and Christian Scriptures and consequently between Jewish and Christian tradition. McFague, on the other hand, dilutes the authority that has been traditionally associated with the Bible and professes a willingness to discard any part of the Scriptures that is no longer "relevant" to the contemporary situation. Some would recognize an implied Antisemitism in this position. For futher insight into this question see Fokkelien van Dijk-Hemmes, "Feminist Theology and Anti-Judaism in the

narrow interpretations of the Jesus event that, in particular, have limited the role of women. She leads the way by recovering the wisdom tradition from its place of neglect and reclaiming it in the name of all the oppressed. While continuing to take a christocentric Christian position, which recognizes the uniqueness of Jesus Christ, Johnson is open to the wisdom to be found in dialogue with other world religions. At the same time she sees the retrieval of wisdom as one more critique of the androcentric nature of Christianity and so challenges theologians to incorporate a non-hierarchical approach to all of life on the planet and thus to liberate all the oppressed. Recently Johnson has turned her attention to cosmology. In her presidential address to the Catholic Theological Society of America she called for the completion of the anthropological turn to the subject by a turning to "the entire interconnected community of life and the network of life-systems in which the human race is embedded, all of which has its own intrinsic value before God."[5] It is her hope and vision for theology that cosmology become a framework and a partner for theological interpretation. This move will have a dramatic impact on the understanding of salvation.

In her understanding of salvation Johnson also seeks to expand theology's current vision. Where McFague stretches the notion of salvation to include all life on the planet, Johnson expands the traditional notion of salvation in the Christian tradition beyond its association with Jesus' death and resurrection to include his life and ministry. Jesus offers the presence of God in the contingency of history and the cosmic Christ, whose spirit supersedes the earthly Jesus, is continually present in this world offering universal salvation.

It is apparent from the preceding reflections that this mutually productive dialogue, which has raised important questions for the future of christological research, moves to an irresolvable difference regarding the status of divinity that has traditionally been attributed

---

Netherlands," *JFSR* 7 (1991) 117–123; Asphodel P. Long, "Anti-Judaism in Britain," *JFSR* 7 (1991) 125–133; Judith Plaskow, "Feminist Anti-Judaism and the Christian God," *JFSR* 7 (1991) 99–108; Leonore Siegele-Wenschkewitz, "The Discussion of Anti-Judaism in Feminist Theology—A New Area of Jewish-Christian Dialogue," *JFSR* 7 (1991) 95–98.

5. "Turn to the Heavens and the Earth: Retrieval of the Cosmos in Theology," in Judith A. Dwyer, ed., CTSA *Proceedings* 51 (1996) 1–14, at 1.

to Jesus. It is because this issue is considered so central to the teachings of Christianity that I have concluded that Sallie McFague's theology verges on post-Christian feminism.

Contributions to Christology

Both these insightful and intelligent women theologians make a significant contribution to ongoing christological study. First of all, in the shared vision of feminist theology they have taken us one step farther toward the full recognition of the cohumanity of women and men signified in the life, death, and resurrection of Jesus of Nazareth. They have responded creatively to Rosemary Radford Ruether's now famous question, "Can a male savior save women?"[6] They answer the question with a resounding "yes." It is possible, they demonstrate clearly, to do christology in a way that reverences the significance of women within the tradition.

McFague and Johnson have both stretched the traditional outer limits of christology and soteriology, pressing toward ecological responsibility and a new vision of universal salvation that brings us into dialogue with other world religions. Specifically, McFague has offered a retrieval of the significance of metaphor for understanding theology and christology, expanding the horizon of our use of religious language. She has insisted that christology look at the role of Christ in relation to nuclear issues and ecological concerns. Johnson has provided a powerful retrieval of the wisdom tradition, shaking up our traditional interpretation of the ontological significance of Jesus' gender and forcing a look at the broader question of Jesus' shared humanity.[7] She has achieved this without relinquishing the uniqueness of Christ to Christianity.

---

6. *Sexism and God-Talk: Toward a Feminist Theology* (Boston: Beacon, 1983) 116–138.

7. It should be noted that Johnson's critical retrieval of the Sophia tradition has been criticized by other feminist scholars. In particular, Elisabeth Schüssler Fiorenza charges that Johnson has not gone far enough. She claims that "a feminist theological discussion of the sophialogical traces in Christian Scriptures that does not at the same time critically evaluate femininity reinscribes the Western sex/gender system." *Jesus. Miriam's Child, Sophia's Prophet: Critical Issues in Feminist Christology* (New York: Continuum, 1994) 160. See also Ben Witherington III, *Jesus the Sage: The Pilgrimage of Wisdom* (Minneapolis: Fortress, 1994) 43.

Moreover, McFague and Johnson alike have demonstrated their prowess as feminist theologians and gained the respect and admiration of their colleagues, thus advancing the work of christology through their evocative work. Feminist christology, as an essential component of the entire field of christological study, can no longer be ignored, for these dynamic women have made it mainline.

Future Questions

Neither Sallie McFague nor Elizabeth A. Johnson would be satisfied to end the discussion here. There remains much work to be done in the field of christology. First of all, the question of Christ's uniqueness has not been entirely resolved. As women continue to ask questions regarding relationship and mutuality, can Christian tradition continue to maintain Christ's unique status? Will the ongoing concerns of feminist theology lead necessarily to a post-Christian position?

Much more needs to be said about the role of the Spirit of Christ who continues to be active in this world on our behalf. Like the concerns of women and their experience, the Spirit has also been neglected in the tradition.

Most of the questions that have been addressed in this study have centered on the concerns of white, middle-class, educated women. There is need for continuing conversation with women from other economic, political, educational, cultural, and religious perspectives.

Last, but not finally, there is continuing need to make this research accessible and meaningful to the common person. That calls for a greater emphasis on the spiritual dimension of these academic concerns. We must have in Jesus one who is indeed like us (women and men) in all things.

Bibliography

Anderson, James Francis. *Reflections on the Analogy of Being.* The Hague: M. Nijhoff, 1967.

Anderson, Ray S. "The Incarnation of God in Feminist Christology" in Alvin F. Kimel, ed., *Speaking the Christian God: The Holy Trinity and the Challenge of Feminism.* Grand Rapids: Eerdmans, 1992, 288–312.

Araya, Victorio. *God of the Poor: The Mystery of God in Latin America.* Maryknoll, N.Y.: Orbis, 1987.

Brock, Rita Nakashima. "A Feminist Consciousness Looks at Christology," *Encounter* 41 (1980) 319–331.

_____. *Journeys by Heart: A Christology of Erotic Power.* New York: Crossroad, 1992.

Brommell, David. "Sallie McFague's Metaphorical Theology." *Journal of the American Academy of Religion* 61 (1993) 485–503.

Brown, Raymond E. *The Gospel According to John I-XII.* Garden City, N.Y.: Doubleday, 1966.

Burrell, David. *Analogy and Philosophical Language.* New Haven: Yale University Press, 1973.

_____. *Exercises in Religious Understanding.* Notre Dame: University of Notre Dame Press, 1974.

Camp, Claudia. "Woman Wisdom as Root Metaphor: A Theological Consideration," in Kenneth G. Hoglund, Elizabeth F. Huwiler, Jonathan T. Glass, and Roger W. Lee, eds., *The Listening Heart: Essays in Wisdom and the Psalms in Honor of Roland E. Murphy, O. Carm. Journal for the Study of the Old Testament.* Supplement Series 58. Sheffield: JSOT Press, 1987, 45–76.

Carr, Anne. "The God Who Is Involved," *Theology Today* 38 (1981) 314–328.

_____ *Transforming Grace: Christian Tradition and Women's Experience.* San Francisco: Harper & Row, 1988.

Carr, Anne, and Elizabeth Schüssler Fiorenza, eds. *The Special Nature of Women. Concilium* 6. Philadelphia: Trinity Press International, 1991.

Carr, Anne, and Elizabeth Schüssler Fiorenza, eds. *Women, Work and Poverty. Concilium: Religion in the Eighties.* Edinburgh: T&T Clark, 1987.

Carroll, B. Jill. "Models of God or Models of Us? On the Theology of Sallie McFague," *Encounter* 52 (1991) 183–196.

Chapman, G. Clarke. "Speaking of God in a Nuclear Age," *Anglican Theological Review* 73 (1991) 250–266.

Chopp, Rebecca S. "Feminism's Theological Pragmatics: A Social Naturalism of Women's Experience," *Journal of Religion* 67 (1987) 239–256.

_____. *The Praxis of Suffering: An Interpretation of Liberation and Political Theologies*. Maryknoll, N.Y.: Orbis, 1986.

_____. *The Power To Speak: Feminism, Language, God*. New York: Crossroad, 1991.

Christ, Carol P. "Embodied Thinking: Reflections on Feminist Theological Method," *Journal of Feminist Studies in Religion* 5 (1989) 7–16.

Christ, Carol P. and Judith Plaskow, eds. *Womanspirit Rising: A Feminist Reader in Religion*. New York: Harper & Row, 1979.

Darling-Smith, Barbara. "A Feminist Christological Exploration," in Ruy O. Costa, ed., *One Faith, Many Cultures: Inculturation, Indigenization, and Contextualization*. The Boston Theological Institute Annual 2. Maryknoll, N.Y.: Orbis, 1988, 71–79.

Davaney, Sheila Greeve. "Directions in Historicism: Language, Experience, and Pragmatic Adjudication," *Zygon* 26 (1991) 201–220.

_____. "Options in Post-Modern Theology," *Dialog* 26 (1987) 196–200.

_____. "Problems with Feminist Theory: Historicity and the Search for Sure Foundations," in Paula M. Cooey, Sharon A. Farmer and Mary Ellen Ross, eds., *Embodied Love: Sensuality and Relationship as Feminist Values*. San Francisco: Harper & Row, 1987, 79–95.

Davaney, Sheila Greeve, ed. *Feminism and Process Thought: The Harvard Divinity School Claremont Center for Process Studies Symposium Papers*. New York: Edwin Mellen, 1978.

Davaney, Sheila Greeve, and John Boswell Cobb, Jr. "Models of God: Theology for an Ecological, Nuclear Age," *Religious Studies Review* 16 (1990) 36–42.

D'Costa, Gavin. *Theology and Religious Pluralism: The Challenge of Other Religions*. Oxford: Basil Blackwell, 1986.

_____, ed. *Christian Uniqueness Reconsidered: The Myth of a Pluralistc Theology of Religions*. Faith Meets Faith Series. Maryknoll, N.Y.: Orbis, 1990.

Dulles, Avery. *Models of Revelation*. New York: Doubleday, 1983.

Dunn, James D. G. *Christology in the Making: A New Testament Inquiry into the Origins of the Doctrine of the Incarnation*. Philadelphia: Westminster, 1990.

Fontaine, Carole. "The Personification of Wisdom," *Harper's Bible Commentary*. San Francisco: Harper & Row, 1988, 501–503.

Gary, William. "Wisdom Christology in the New Testament: Its Scope and Relevance." *Theology* 89 (1986) 448–459.

Gilkey, Langdon. *Gilkey on Tillich.* New York: Crossroad, 1990.

_____. *Naming the Whirlwind: The Renewal of God-Language.* Indianapolis and New York: Bobbs-Merrill, 1969.

Grant, Jacquelyn. "Womanist Theology: Black Women's Experience as a Source of Doing Theology, With Special Reference to Christology," *Journal of the Interdenominational Theological Center* 13 (1986) 195–212.

Green, Garrett. "Reconstructing Christian Theology." *Religious Studies Review* 9 (1983) 219–222.

Haight, Roger. *An Alternative Vision.* New York: Paulist, 1985.

Hammet, Jenny Yates. *Woman's Transformations: A Psychological Theology.* Symposium Series 8. New York: Edwin Mellen, 1982.

Hampson, Daphne, and Rosemary Radford Ruether. "Is There a Place for Feminists in a Christian Church?" *New Blackfriars* 68 (1987) 7–24.

Hellwig, Monika. *Jesus, the Compassion of God.* Theology and Life Series 9. Wilmington, Del.: Michael Glazier, 1985.

_____. "Re-emergence of the Human, Critical, Public Jesus," *Theological Studies* 50 (1989) 466–480.

Heyward, Carter. "Suffering, Redemption, and Christ: Shifting the Grounds of Feminist Christology," *Christianity and Crisis: A Christian Journal of Opinion* 49 (1989) 381–386.

_____. *The Redemption of God: A Theology of Mutual Relation.* New York: University Press of America, 1982.

Hick, John, and Paul F. Knitter, eds. *The Myth of Christian Uniqueness: Toward a Pluralistic Theology of Religions.* Faith Meets Faith Series. Maryknoll, N.Y.: Orbis, 1987.

Hilkert, Mary Catherine, O.P. "Feminist Theology: A Review of the Literature," *Theological Studies* 56 (1995) 327–352.

Hines, Mary E., Mary Rose D'Angelo, and John Carmody. "Three perspectives: *She Who Is: The Mystery of God in Feminist Theological Discourse,*" *Horizons* 20 (1993) 339–344.

Hoffman, John C. "Metaphorical or Narrative Theology," *Studies in Religion* 16 (1987) 173–185.

Imbelli, Robert P. "*She Who Is*: A Review," *Church* 51 (1993) 51–56.

Jeanrond, Werner, and Jennifer L. Rife, eds. *Radical Pluralism and Truth: David Tracy and the Hermeneutics of Religion.* New York: Crossroad, 1991.

Johnson, Elizabeth A. "Analogy/Doxology and Their Connection with Christology in the Thought of Wolfhart Pannenberg." Ph.D. dissertation. The Catholic University of America, 1981.

_____. "Between the Times: Religious Life and the Postmodern Experience of God." *Review for Religious* 53 (1994) 6–28.

_____. *Consider Jesus: Waves of Renewal in Christology.* New York: Crossroad, 1991.

_____. "Does God Play Dice? Divine Providence and Chance." *Theological Studies* 57 (1996) 3–18.

_____. "Don't Make Mary the Feminist Face of God." *U. S. Catholic* (1994) 30–32.

_____. *Feminism and Sharing the Faith: A Catholic Dilemma.* Warren Lecture Series in Catholic Studies 29. Tulsa: The University of Tulsa, 1994.

_____. "Feminist Hermeneutics," *Chicago Studies* 27 (1988) 123–135.

_____. "The Incomprehensibility of God and the Image of God Male and Female." *Theological Studies* 45 (1984) 441–465.

_____. "Jesus and Salvation," in Paul Crowley, ed., The Catholic Theological Society of America, *Proceedings* 49 (1994) 1–18.

_____. "Jesus, the Wisdom of God: A Biblical Basis for Non-androcentric Christology," *Ephemerides Theologicae Lovanienses* 16 (1985) 261–294.

_____. "Jesus Christ in the Catechism," *America* 162 (1990) 206–208; 221–222.

_____. "The Legitimacy of the God Question: Pannenberg's Anthropology," *Irish Theological Quarterly* 52 (1986) 289–303.

_____. "Lutheran/Roman Catholic Dialogue Achieves Statement on the One Mediator, the Saints and Mary," *Ecumenical Trends* 19 (1990) 97–101.

_____. "The Maleness of Christ," in Anne Carr and Elizabeth Schüssler Fiorenza, eds., *The Special Nature of Women? Concilium* 6. Philadelphia: Trinity Press International, 1991, 108–116.

_____. "Marian Devotion in the Western Church," in Jill Raitt, Bernard McGinn and John Meyendorff, eds., *Christian Spirituality: High Middle Ages and Reformation.* New York: Crossroad, 1987, 392–414.

_____. "The Marian Tradition and the Reality of Women," *Horizons* 12 (1985) 116–135.

_____. "Mary and Contemporary Christology: Rahner and Schillebeeckx," *Eglies et Theologie* (Ottawa) 15 (1984) 155–182.

_____. "Mary and the Female Face of God," *Theological Studies* 50 (1989) 500–526.

_____. "May We Invoke the Saints Today?" *Theology Today* 44 (1987) 32–52.

_____. "The Ongoing Christology of Wolfhart Pannenberg," *Horizons* 9 (1982) 237–250.

_____. "Redeeming the Name of Christ: Christology," in Catherine Mowry LaCugna, ed., *Freeing Theology: The Essentials of Theology in Feminist Perspective.* San Francisco: Harper Collins, 1993, 115–137.

_____. "Resurrection: Promise of the Future," *Sisters Today* 67/6 (1995) 404–411.

_____. Review of *Models of God: Theology for an Ecological, Nuclear Age* by Sallie McFague. *Commonweal* 115 (1988) 151–152.

_____. "The Right Way to Speak About God: Pannenberg on Analogy," *Theological Studies* 43 (1982) 673–692.

_____. "Saints and Mary," in Francis Schüssler Fiorenza and John P. Galvin, eds., *Systematic Theology: Roman Catholic Perspectives.* Minneapolis: Fortress, 1991, 2:145–177.

_____. "The Search for the Living God," *Grail* 10 (1994) 11–29.

_____. *She Who Is: The Mystery of God in Feminist Theological Discourse.* New York: Crossroad, 1992.

_____. "The Symbolic Character of Theological Statements About Mary." *Journal of Ecumenical Studies* 22 (1985) 312–335.

_____. "A Theological Case for God-she: Expanding the Treasury of Metaphor," *Commonweal* 120 (1993) 9–22.

_____. "The Theological Relevance of the Historical Jesus: A Debate and a Thesis." *The Thomist* 48 (1984) 1–43.

_____. "Turn to the Heavens and the Earth: Retrieval of the Cosmos in Theology," Presidential Address, The Catholic Theological Society of America. *Proceedings of the Fifty-first Annual Convention* 51 (1996) 1–14.

_____. "Who Is the Holy Spirit?" *Catholic Update* (June, 1995) 1–4.

_____. "Wisdom Was Made Flesh and Pitched Her Tent Among Us," in Maryanne Stevens, ed., *Reconstructing The Christ Symbol: Essays in Feminist Christology.* New York: Paulist, 1993, 95–117.

_____. *Women, Earth, and Creator Spirit*, 1993 Madeleva Lecture in Spirituality. New York: Paulist, 1993.

Johnson, Elizabeth A., Susan A. Ross, and Mary Catherine Hilkert, O.P., "Feminist Theology: A Review of Literature." *Theological Studies* 56 (1995) 327–352.

Kaufman, Gordon D. "Constructing the Concept of God," in Axel D. Steuer and James Wm. McClendon, Jr., eds., *Is God God?* Nashville: Abingdon, 1973, 111–143.

_____. *An Essay on Theological Method.* Missoula: Scholars Press, 1975; rev. ed. 1979.

_____. *In Face of Mystery: A Constructive Theology.* Cambridge, Mass.: Harvard University Press, 1993.

_____. "The Influence of Feminist Theory on my Theological Work," *Journal of Feminist Studies in Religion* 7 (1991) 95–127.

_____. "Models of God: Is Metaphor Enough?" *Religion & Intellectual Life* 5 (1988) 11–18.

_____. "Reconceiving God for a Nuclear Age," in Leroy S. Rouner, ed., *Knowing Religiously*. Notre Dame, Ind.: University of Notre Dame Press, 1984, 133–149.

_____. *The Theological Imagination: Constructing the Concept of God*. Philadelphia: Westminster, 1981.

_____. *Theology for a Nuclear Age*. Philadelphia: Westminster, 1985.

Kimel, Alvin F., Jr., ed. *Speaking The Christian God: The Holy Trinity and the Challenge of Feminism*. Grand Rapids: Eerdmans, 1992.

Kliever, Lonnie. "Alternative Conceptions of Religion as a Symbol System," *Union Seminary Quarterly Review* 27 (1972) 91–102.

Knitter, Paul F. "Christian Salvation: Its Nature and Uniqueness—An Inter-religious Proposal," *New Theology Review* 7 (1994) 33–46.

_____. *No Other Name? A Critical Survey of Christian Attitudes Toward the World Religions*. American Society of Missiology Series 7. Maryknoll, N.Y.: Orbis, 1985.

_____, ed. *Pluralism and Oppression: Theology in World Perspective*. College Theology Society 24. New York: University Press of America, 1988.

Lilburne, Geoffrey R. "Christology in Dialogue with Feminism," *Horizons* 11 (1984) 7–27.

Loades, Ann, ed. *Feminist Theology: A Reader*. London: S.P.C.K.; Louisville: Westminster/John Knox, 1990.

Long, Asphodel P. "Anti-Judaism in Britain," *Journal of Feminist Studies in Religion* 7 (1991) 125–133.

Malone, Nancy. "A Discussion of Sallie McFague's Models of God," *Religion and Intellectual Life* 5 (1988) 9–44.

McAvoy, Jane. "God-talk: Three Modern Approaches," *Lexington Theological Quarterly* 22 (1987) 106–117.

McFague, Sallie. *The Body of God: An Ecological Theology*. Minneapolis: Fortress, 1993.

_____. "Conversion: Life on the Edge of the Raft." *Interpretation* 32 (1978) 255–268.

_____. "Cosmology and Christianity: Implications of the Common Creation Story for Theology," in Sheila Greeve Davaney, ed., *Theology at the End of Modernity: Essays in Honor of Gordon D. Kaufman*. Philadelphia: Trinity Press International, 1991, 19–40.

_____. "An Earthly Theological Agenda," *The Christian Century* 108 (1991) 12–15.

_____. "An Epilogue: The Christian Paradigm," in Peter C. Hodgson and Robert H. King, eds., *Christian Theology: An Introduction to its Traditions and Tasks*. Philadelphia: Fortress, 1982, 323–336.

_____. "The Ethic of God as Mother, Lover and Friend," in Ann Loades, ed., *Feminist Theology: A Reader*. Louisville: Westminster/John Knox, 1990, 255–274.

_____. "God as Mother," in Judith Plaskow and Carol P. Christ, eds., *Weaving the Visions: New Patterns in Feminist Spirituality*. San Francisco: Harper & Row, 1989, 139–150.

_____. "Ian Barbour: Theologian's Friend, Scientist's Interpreter," *Zygon* 31 (1996) 21–28.

_____. "Imaginary Gardens with Real Toads: Realism in Fiction and Theology," *Semeia* 13 (1978) 241–261.

_____. "Imaging a Theology of Nature: The World as God's Body," in Charles Birch, William Eakin, and Jay B. McDaniel, eds., *Liberating Life: Contemporary Approaches to Ecological Theology*. Maryknoll, N.Y.: Orbis, 1990, 201–227.

_____. *Literature and the Christian Life*. New Haven: Yale University Press, 1986.

_____. *Metaphorical Theology: Models of God in Religious Language*. Philadelphia: Fortress, 1982.

_____. *Models of God: Theology for an Ecological, Nuclear Age*. Philadelphia: Fortress, 1987.

_____. "Mother God," in Anne Carr and Elizabeth Schüssler Fiorenza, eds., *Motherhood: Experience, Institution, Theology. Concilium: Religion in the Eighties*. Edinburgh: T & T Clark, 1989, 138–143.

_____. "Parable, Metaphor, and Theology," *Journal of the American Academy of Religion* 42 (1974) 630–645.

_____. Review of *Plurality and Ambiguity: Hermeneutics, Religion, Hope*, by David Tracy. *Theology Today* 44 (1988) 500–503.

_____. *Speaking in Parables: A Study in Metaphor and Theology*. Philadelphia: Fortress, 1975.

_____. "A Square in the Quilt: One Theologian's Contribution to the Planetary Agenda," in Steven C. Rockefeller and John C. Elder, eds., *An Interfaith Dialogue, Spirit and Nature: Why the Environment is a Religious Issue*. Boston: Beacon, 1992, 39–58.

_____. "The World as God's Body," *The Christian Century* 105 (1988) 671–673.

Moulder, James. "Why Feminist Theology Encourages Unbelief," in Johan Mouton, Andries van Aarde, and William Vorster, eds., *Paradigms and Progress in Theology*. Pretoria: Human Sciences Research Council, 1988, 252–258.

Murphy, Roland A. *The Tree of Life: An Exploration of Biblical Wisdom Literature*. Anchor Bible Reference Library. New York: Doubleday, 1990.

Nunn, Madelon. "Christology or Male-olatry?" *The Duke Divinity School Review* 42 (1977) 143–148.

O'Connor, June. "Feminism and the Christ," in Linda J. Tressier, ed., *Concepts of the Ultimate*. New York: St. Martin's, 1989, 59-79.

O'Neill, Mary Aquin, and Mary McClintock Fulkerson. Review of *She Who Is: The Mystery of God in Feminist Theological Discourse. Religious Studies Review* 21 (1995) 19–25.

Pauw, Amy Plantinga. "Braiding a New Footbridge: Christian Wisdom, Classic and Feminist," *The Christian Century* 110 (1993) 1159–1162.

Penn, Ray C. "Competing Hermeneutical Foundations and Religious Communication: Why Protestants Can't Understand Each Other." *The Journal of Communication and Religion* 11 (1998) 10–21.

Perkins, Pheme. "Jesus: God's Wisdom," *Word and World: Theology for Christian Ministry* 7 (1987) 273–280.

Peters, Ted. "McFague's Metaphors," *Dialog* 27 (1988) 131–140.

Plaskow, Judith. "Feminist Anti-Judaism and the Christian God," *Journal of Feminist Studies in Religion* 7 (1991) 99–108.

Rahner, Karl. *Foundations of Christian Faith*, translated by William Dych. New York: Seabury, 1978.

_____. "The Theology of Symbol," *Theological Investigations* 4, translated by Kevin Smyth. New York: Seabury, 1974, 221–252.

Richter, Blake K. "Recent Views of the Revelatory Character of the Bible and Their Implications for Its Interpretation." D.Min. Thesis. San Anselmo: San Francisco Theological Seminary, 1993.

Ritchie, Nelly. "Women and Christology," in D. Kirkpatrick, ed., *Faith Born in the Struggle for Life*. Grand Rapids: Eerdmans, 1988, 84–97.

Ricouer, Paul. "Biblical Hermeneutics," *Semeia* 4 (1975) 29–148.

_____. *The Metaphorical Process*. Toronto: The University of Toronto Press, 1975.

Ruether, Rosemary Radford. *To Change the World: Christology and Cultural Criticism*. New York: Crossroad, 1991.

_____. "*Imago Dei*, Christian Tradition and Feminist Hermeneutics," in Kari Elisabeth Börresen, ed., *Image of God and Gender Models in Judaeo-Christian Tradition*. Oslo: Solum Förlag, 1991, 258–281.

_____. "The Liberation of Christology from Patriarchy," *Religion and Intellectual Life* 2 (1985) 116–128.

_____. *Sexism and God-Talk: Toward a Feminist Theology*. Boston: Beacon, 1983.

_____. "The Task of Feminist Theology," in John D. Woodbridge and Thomas Edward McComiskey, eds., *Doing Theology in Today's World: Essays in Honor of Kenneth S. Kantzer*. Grand Rapids: Zondervan, 1991, 359–376.

Santmire, Paul H. "Toward a New Theology of Nature," *Dialog* 25 (1986) 43–50.

Schroten, Egbert. "'Playing God' Some Theological Comments on Metaphor," in John D. Woodbridge and Thomas Edward McComiskey, eds.,*Christian Faith and Philosophical Theology: Essays in Honour of Vincent Brümme*. Grand Rapids: Zondervan, 1991, 359–376.

Schüssler Fiorenza, Elisabeth. *But She Said: Feminist Practices of Biblical Interpretation*. Boston: Beacon, 1992.

_____. "Changing Paradigms," *The Christian Century* 107 (1990) 796–800.

_____. *Jesus. Miriam's Child, Sophia's Prophet: Critical Issues in Feminist Christology*. New York: Continuum, 1994.

_____. *In Memory of Her: A Feminist Theological Reconstruction of Christian Origins*. New York: Crossroad, 1983.

Schüssler Fiorenza, Francis. *Foundational Theology: Jesus and the Church*. New York: Crossroad, 1984.

Scobie, Charles H. H. "The Place of Wisdom in Biblical Theology," *Biblical Theology Bulletin* 14 (1984) 43–47.

Scott, R. B. "The Study of the Wisdom Literature." *Interpretation* 24 (1970) 20–45.

Sharpe, Kevin J. "Theological Method and Gordon Kaufman," *Religious Studies* 15 (1979) 173–190.

Siegele-Wenschkewitz, Leonore. "The Discussion of Anti-Judaism In Feminist Theology—A New Area of Jewish-Christian Dialogue," *Journal of Feminist Studies in Religion* 7 (1991) 95–98.

Sobrino, Jon. "The Experience of God in the Church of the Poor," in *The True Church and the Poor*, translated by Matthew O'Connell. Maryknoll, N.Y.: Orbis, 1984.

Sontag, Frederick. "Metaphorical Non-Sequitur?" *Scottish Journal of Theology* 44 (1991) 1–18.

Soskice, Janet Martin. *Metaphor and Religious Language*. New York: Oxford University Press, 1985.

Thistlethwaite, Susan B. "God and Her Survival in a Nuclear Age," *Journal of Feminist Studies in Religion* 4 (1988) 73–88.

Tillich, Paul. *Dynamics of Faith*. New York: Harper & Row, 1957.

_____. "The Meaning and Justification of Religious Symbols" and "The Religious Symbol" in Sidney Hook, ed., *Religious Experience and Truth*. New York: New York University Press, 1961, 3–11; 301–321.

_____. *Systematic Theology*, vols 1–3. Chicago: University of Chicago Press, 1951–1963.

_____. *Theology of Culture*. New York: Oxford University Press, 1959.

Tracy, David. *The Analogical Imagination: Christian Theology and the Culture of Pluralism.* New York: Crossroad, 1981.

_____. "Author's Response," Review Symposium on *The Analogical Imagination. Horizons* 8 (1981) 329–339.

_____. *Blessed Rage for Order: The New Pluralism in Theology.* New York: Seabury, 1975.

_____. "Metaphor and Religion: The Test Case of Christian Texts," in Sheldon Sacks, ed., *On Metaphor.* Chicago: The University of Chicago Press, 1979, 89–104.

_____. "Revisionist Practical Theology and the Meaning of Public Discourses," *Pastoral Psychology* 26 (1977) 83–94.

Van Dijk-Hemmes, Fokkelien. "Feminist Theology and Anti-Judaism in the Netherlands," *Journal of Feminist Studies in Religion* 7 (1991) 117–123.

Walker, Megan. "The Challenge of Feminism to the Christian Concept of God," *Journal of Theology for Southern Africa* 66 (1989) 4–20.

Wells, Harold G. "Trinitarian Feminism: Elizabeth Johnson's Wisdom Christology," *Theology Today* 52 (1995) 330–343.

Wilckens, Ulrich. "Sophia," in Gerhard Kittel and Gerhard Friedrich, eds., *Theological Dictionary of the New Testament* 10 vols. (Grand Rapids: Eerdmans, 1964–1976) 7:465–528.

Williamson, Raymond Keith. *Introduction to Hegel's Philosophy of Religion.* Albany, N.Y.: SUNY Press, 1984.

Wilson-Kastner, Patricia. *Faith, Feminism, and the Christ.* Philadelphia: Fortress, 1983.

Witherington, Ben III. *Jesus the Sage: The Pilgrimage of Wisdom.* Minneapolis: Fortress, 1994.

Young, Pamela Dickey. "Diversity in Feminist Christology," *Studies in Religion* 21 (1992) 81–90.

Young, Robin Darling. "She Who Is: Who Is She?" *The Thomist* 58 (1994) 323–333.

Zeigler, Leslie. "Christianity or Feminism?" in Alvin F. Kimel, Jr., ed., *Speaking the Christian God: The Holy Trinity and the Challenge of Feminism.* Grand Rapids: Eerdmans, 1992, 313–334.

Index